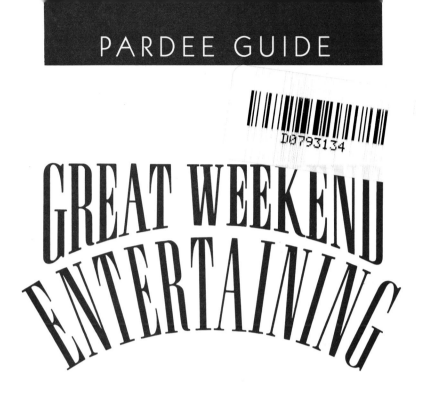

D0793134

GREAT WEEKEND ENTERTAINING

GREAT WEEKEND ENTERTAINING

AN ESSENTIAL COMPANION FOR FUN-LOVING HOSTS AND GUESTS

BETTIE BEARDEN PARDEE

PEACHTREE PUBLISHERS, LTD.
Atlanta

*To you, my friends, near and far—
who have been both favorite guest
and thoughtful host—
I dedicate this book with fond memories.*

Published by
PEACHTREE PUBLISHERS, LTD.
494 Armour Circle, NE
Atlanta, Georgia 30324

© 1991 Bettie Bearden Pardee
Illustrations © 1991 Cynthia Carrozza

Cover design by Jennifer Ellison
Cover illustration and interior illustrations by Cynthia Carrozza
Interior design by Candace J. Magee
Composition by Kathryn D. Mothershed

Manufactured in the United States of America

10 9 8 7 6 5 4 3 2 1

Library of Congress Cataloging in Publication Data

Pardee, Bettie Bearden
Great weekend entertaining / Bettie Bearden Pardee.
p. cm. -- (Pardee guide)
Includes index.
ISBN 1-56145-022-7 : $9.95
1. Entertaining. 2. Hospitality. 3. Games. 4. Parties.
I. Title. II. Series : Pardee, Bettie Bearden   Pardee guide.
GV1472.7.W4P37   1991
793.2--dc20
90-28261
CIP

CONTENTS

III. Social Circumstances

IV. Weekend "To Do's"

V. A Sampling of Great Weekend Parties

Introduction

What never lets us down, buoys us up for inevitable Mondays and arrives 52 times a year?
Ah, WEEKENDS . . . .

And rent or own, spacious or miniscule, seashore or mountain, eager guest or heart-attack hostess . . . weekends and entertaining go together.

You might perceive that this book is written for hosts, and guests, whose weekend retreats don't come with hot and cold running servants. That's why, underlying the hints, how-to's and shortcuts, I've aimed for a general sense of levity—precisely the quality that we all hope to associate with weekend entertaining. Because for me, 24-hour cohabitation is challenging enough with my beloved, much less with friends and acquaintances. That dash for the last *hot* shower or a hovering guest who remains underfoot can strain even devoted friendships.

The pure truth of the matter is that hosting a house party should be FUN. And being a houseguest should be FUN, too. Yes, living in "altered states of connubial bliss" does take some work on both sides. But an understanding of some simple practicalities will smooth the way for the good times that we all anticipate in our weekends—complete with the thrill of new climes, a change of routine and an escape from weekday demands. Plus the opportunity to relax the day long or dance the night away.

So, step into my book and ENJOY.

Oh, yes . . . a bit of advice that has made weekend entertaining (and marriage) easier for me . . .

> "Let there be spaces in your togetherness."
> Kahil Gibran, *The Prophet*

The ABC'S of Weekend Entertaining

"**A**re we having fun yet?!" Battle cry of a relentless host.

Barbecue. Every smart host's summer kitchen.

Children. Sure they're invited?

Dripping faucets? Beware—cold water stains the porcelain, hot water costs you money.

Evening star . . . and all the others that you can see so clearly.

Fish. One of God's creatures to whom a guest bears a strong resemblance after three days.

"**G**ee . . . I've never seen a tarantula in my bed before."

House party. Altered states of connubial bliss.

"**I** bet you thought we were coming Friday."

Jams and jellies. Great house gifts—especially if you made them.

Kibitz. What you do with good friends.

Laughter. Let there be a lot of it in your weekends.

Mosquitoes. An uninvited hanger-on that can really get under your skin.

Not another scheduled event?!

Offer to help—even if you don't mean it.

Picnic. Portables that won't hamper you.

Quick departures, on time, with nothing left behind.

Rules of the house. Mind them . . . they make for smoother relations.

Sunburned and seasick, but not sorry you came.

Tipping the staff? Not 'til you've checked with the host first.

Uninvited guest? An oxymoron—if you weren't invited you're an interloper, not a guest.

Veni, vidi, vici—the guest who won't be returning.

Wellies belong in your closet, not under the living room chair.

X-actly which bathroom is mine?

"**Y**'all come back, y'heah?" Traditional southern send-off.

Zip-lock bags. They make moveable feasts possible.

Everything I Need to Know About House Parties I Learned at Camp

Camp life is a microcosm of our culture—those seemingly innocuous "character building" experiences of yesteryear linger on to serve us, or haunt us, in our adult lives.

Camp Rule #1
Pack carefully so you won't forget anything—coming or going.

Camp Rule #2
Know exactly when you're supposed to arrive—and when Mom and Dad are supposed to pick you up.

Camp Rule #3
Practice neat and tidy habits.
△ Make your bed with hospital corners.
△ Keep all possessions together and in your camp trunk.
△ Leave the bathroom clean.
△ Wet bathing suits go in a plastic bag, not on the blanket.

Camp Rule #4
Be enthusiastic about activities that have been planned (including Bunk Skit Night).
And be on time.

Camp Rule #5
Eat what you are served or say, "No, thank you."
Don't raid the kitchen or the icebox.

Camp Rule #6
Good sportsmanship is its own reward . . . whether you're a guppie or a porpoise.

Camp Rule #7
Honor the "Good Camper's Code."
△ Offer to help.
△ Don't drop soft drink cans or candy wrappers in the woods.
△ Don't play your radio during rest period.
△ When you phone Mom and Dad, call collect.
△ When it's time to leave, take the sheets off your bed.

GREAT WEEKEND ENTERTAINING

I

GUESTING GAMES

GUESTING GAMES

15-No-Make-That-20-Ways-to-Make Weekend-Entertaining-Easier

It only happens once (if you're lucky). Those I'm-so-excited-I've-got-a-vacation-house-I've-invited-everyone-I-know blues. Better known as the "honeymoon year." To you, these observations and tips are dedicated.

But even the practiced host and hostess confess to pursuing and perfecting ways to make weekend entertaining easier. *After all, a weekend is actually a 48- to 72-hour party by another name.* If you don't shift into a lower gear than the one you adopt for a party back home, you're going to crash and burn at the end of the first season. This ability to shift gears and stay flexible is a weekend host's greatest ally. Others that bear consideration:

1. Invite people who enjoy the kind of life *you* like.

2. Invite people who don't "wear thin" (a wonderful dinner partner does not always a great weekender make).

3. Invite people you can make completely comfortable. All guests should be able to coexist happily in the space and place provided.

4. Old school chums and heads of state should be treated exactly the same.

5. Opt for twin beds, not double or queen. No one minds "splitting up" for a night or two, but many abhor having to sleep together—especially strangers.

6. Put your freezer to work for you. Cook every weekday meal with future weekend entertaining in mind. Prepare additional quantities for freezing ahead.

7. Avoid feeding guests three *square* meals a day—let everyone be on their own for breakfast, or have a picnic for lunch, or go out for dinner (if for no other reason than variety).

8. To maintain your sanity, offer plenty of ways and means for guests to pass the time—without you.

9. Conversely, always leave time in the day for those guests who wish to go off by themselves.

10. Understand that it is your pleasure to be a hostess—it is *not* your obligation to be a hostage.

11. Have a puzzle going on some table—as an icebreaker, rainy day toy, team sport, for whiling away hours.

12. Write ahead and ask guests what one thing they feel they 1) do very well and 2) don't do very well at all. Not only will you learn some provocative things about your intended guests, but you'll be better prepared when task-assigning time comes.

13. Nine times out of ten, "a busy guest is a happy guest." Involve guests in tasks; don't just leave them standing around with open-ended requests.

14. Tell guests what you would like for them to bring when they ask (unless they're bores, they're going to bring something anyway, so it might as well be something you need).

15. Be realistic and don't overschedule. Guests come to the country/beach/mountains predominantly to:
 —eat and drink
 —take a nap or go to the beach.

16. Try to include one great gourmet who likes to show off his talents in the kitchen.

17. Develop house rules based on *your* lifestyle and proclivities. Your graciousness comes into play after the unwritten understanding "When in Rome . . ."

18. Be specific. Leave nothing to chance—from a printed map and directions to a ferry schedule with "suggested" departure times (underlined, if necessary).

19. BELIEVE that weekends are easier, an escape from hectic weekdays. Everything that you do should be carried out at a "second nature" pace.

20. Avoid a clash of expectations. Sound out guests early on about what pace and activities they are looking forward to versus what you might be planning. Sleeping late and taking afternoon naps might not jibe with early morning fishing and mid-afternoon tennis tournaments.

"To offer hospitality, or to accept it, is but an instinct which man has acquired in the long course of his self-development. Lions do not ask one another to their lairs, nor do birds keep open nest."

—Max Beerbohm

How to Make an Impact

Thoughtful Host—Favorite Guest

Are you a host—or are you a guest?

Facing the question head on—how do you *really* wish to spend your time—will determine whether you are hailed as a *thoughtful* host or a *favorite* guest.

Don't be ambivalent. There's nothing wrong with admitting that you only want to be a guest, who lets others shoulder most of the responsibilities; or, conversely, a host who likes the independence and luxury of planning and doing everything exactly as he or she *wants* it.

And, there are many styles—one host may want to turn himself over to his guests completely, escorting them to museums, accompanying them on shopping sprees, including them in all the social events. While another may mean, sincerely and literally, "mi casa es su casa"—and go on about his life.

Two important tips to remember:

❏ Going away for the weekend is like going on holiday. Guests want to feel pampered and to sense a sincere concern for their personal interests. But avoid fuss, flutter and exaggerated efforts on their behalf. For this only tends to make a houseguest uncomfortable, feeling that his host is being put to a great deal of bother or effort on his account.

❏ Greeting guests with food and drink (no matter what the time of day or night) is an hospitable gesture. And when keyed to local favorites, makes for an even more memorable first impression—a tray of rum drinks after making the long ascent to the villa in Mustique, a bottle of local wine when arriving at the farmhouse in Napa Valley, a bowl of steamers to sate the appetite in Nantucket.

The Thoughtful Host

✦ Carefully orchestrate the guest list to ensure harmony and synergism, while avoiding any entangling alliances that could derail the weekend.

✦ Allow guests to be as independent as possible while still feeling that they are "part of the family" and activities.

✦ Emphasize pre-planning and organization when hosting a group where everyone is a stranger, thereby freeing yourself to mix and "nurse" guests.

✦ Don't treat the weekend like a stay at Club Med, where guests are over-programmed to exhaustion. As one houseguest was heard to comment: "I came to rest, not have a breakdown."

✦ Let guests catch their breath after arriving, particularly if they have had a long or taxing trip; don't schedule social engagements or tasks too close to arrival time.

✦ Ask ahead to see if guests have any other plans during the weekend; otherwise, it is the host's obligation to plan for or provide meals.

✦ Always have nibbles in the fridge, a basket of fruit on the counter, delectables in the cookie jar.

✦ Serve local (and ideally homegrown) fruits and vegetables; introduce guests to native cuisine and regional samplings.

✦ Give explict dress suggestions; otherwise, the guest overpacks with unnecessary clothes "just in case" or risks arriving without needed items.

✦ If accommodations permit, apportion guest rooms according to guest's habits—those who like to party all night or rise early, get one location; the late sleeper or city dweller (who might resent the rural racket of roosters and dogs) is given a secluded room.

- Develop the ability to be composed, self-assured and to take everything in stride.

- Give the weekend a theme. This sets it apart from other weekends, contributes a sense of occasion for guests, affords continuity throughout their stay.

- Always have fresh flowers awaiting a guest in both bedroom and bath.

- Practice nonchalance in the face of accidents or breakage caused by a guest.

- Don't let a situation persist that will embarrass someone, be it a lack of sobriety or spinach in the teeth.

Anecdote

"Taking Care of Details"

The gracious hostess, *sensitive to a female guest's plight of lost luggage on the night of a party, presents her houseguest with a "little black dress." And a large wicker tray laden with a selection of accessories, jewelry and scarves.*

Thoughtful "must-haves" and special gestures on the part of a host—

- Names and locations of bank ATM machines

- Books on the city or locale; copies of pertinent articles on the area

- "To do" options, from art shows to show houses

- Names of "specialists": i.e., personal shopper in New York City; entrée to antique shops and pottery factories

- Copies of rules and scoring for unusual sports (court tennis or bocci) that guests may be "required" to watch

- Current train, ferry, bus schedules

- Fax machine

- List of sitters, kennels, day-care centers

- Shawls, umbrellas, hats, extra bathing suits

- Sotheby, Christie and other art auction catalogs (for guests too tired to read or to inspire the weekend artist)

- Desk equipped with paper, postcards, pens and pencils, stamps, paper clips, small stapler

- Library of paperback bestsellers, hardback classics, magazines on good cross-section of subjects and video selections

---

SHORT SUBJECT

The Lending Library, a much-appreciated detail:
Paperbacks are a particularly thoughtful gesture, as there is not much invested and you can, with great magnanimity, encourage, nay implore, your guests to "take it with you"—with the added and ultimate gracious gesture of "and please do not trouble yourself with the inconvenience of returning it."

On the other hand . . .
As for hardbacks, and particularly newer ones that cost not a small penny, which you would understandably be hesitant to lend, consider this book plate:
"This book has been stolen from the library of _____."

Other Notes on Being a Thoughtful Host

A guest room should be ready at all times so that a host can say, with all sincerity, "We'd love to have you stay"; the guest, in turn, doesn't feel like an imposition. All details should be so well attended that the host never need go in the guest room other than to add fresh flowers.

Asides from a hostess:

"And when it comes to activities . . . nothing is more annoying than a guest who demurs, "I don't care"—and really doesn't mean it!"

. . . and a guest

"A HAPPY GUEST is one who doesn't feel like a burden or a 'thousand questions' nuisance."

SHORT SUBJECT

My vote is for the observant guest . . .
Look and see what you can do, where you can be helpful, without getting in the way. TIMING is important. Knowing *when* to ask is as important as knowing *what* to ask. Don't wear the hostess out with a barrage of offers. Say, "I'm good at X, Y and Z and am ready and willing. When you know what you would like for me to do, just speak up. In the meantime, I'll let you have peace and quiet."

TIP FOR THE YOUNG HOST

Help your guests shine by forewarning them about parental foibles or family cultural ways. Explain that things are done "like this" or house rules dictate that we not _____.

Party planning and giving — There are some real pluses to having a party the day guests arrive . . .

1. The compliment to guests is a good beginning for a weekend.

2. Guests start right in on a festive note, having FUN.

3. The inevitable planning and preparation doesn't interrupt the weekend, with the host having to take time away from guests.

4. And the host has the entire weekend free to be with guests.

5. Guests won't feel obligated to work; the host won't have to keep declining.

6. It sets the stage for party guests to invite hosts and houseguests to other pre-planned weekend events or otherwise help hosts entertain houseguests—"come by for drinks," "join us at the club for lunch," "_____ is in town and I think you might like to meet him."

Host . . . Should your well-intentioned plans find you scheduling the party some time during the weekend, bear one point in mind: A pet peeve of many a guest is spending the majority of their time—when they had planned to vegetate or check out the local sights—working on party details.

Yes, guests should be willing to help. But as a hostess of weekend houseguests, be realistic. Take careful pains with your planning and organization. If you do need help, be courteous. Keep the list *short* and *specific*.

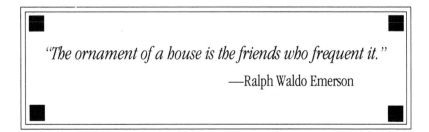

"The ornament of a house is the friends who frequent it."

—Ralph Waldo Emerson

The Favorite Guest

It is your job to make the host forget that you are an imposition—which you are. And though you may be sunburned and flea-bitten, dragged from baseball games to tea parties, overrun by pets and children, the favorite guest remains affable and un-ruffled.

In addition, he or she arrives with gift in hand, telephone credit card in the pocket, pleasant countenance on the face, primed to contribute to the flow and camaraderie of the weekend.

Some other characteristics that will all but assure you are invited back:

❦ Know exactly when you are expected to arrive—and depart.

❦ Don't sit on perishable furnishings in wet bathing suits or sweaty tennis clothes.

❦ The perfect houseguest doesn't act like a guest. Appear comfortable and look for ways to put the host at ease.

❦ Don't come with the flu, dirty laundry or uninvited pets or children.

❦ If asked, respond forthrightly about what you would like to do (spend the afternoon at the beach); what you don't want to do (go sailing); what you are good at (mixing a Caesar salad) and not so good at (mixing a martini).

❦ Accept that it is as much your responsibility as the host's to see that the weekend "works"—polish up your conversation skills, practice your tennis serve, catch up on some good jokes.

❦ Don't make a big, over-blown fuss if you break something; apologize sincerely, clean it up and, if valuable, replace it with its exact, or closest, counterpart ASAP.

❦ Write a thank-you note within two weeks after departure.

❦ Pack smart—and small. Many guest rooms have limited space and can't accommodate a furniture-size suitcase.

Pamperings for the Bed and Bath

As a rule, separate families do not usually live under the same roof, a fact that is thrown out the window come house party time. All the more reason for a host to give very careful thought to that space which a guest may consider his or her "own." That means not only giving thought to creature comforts, but assembling the guest room with the same attention that you would your own master bedroom.

For the best guest rooms are those that are an extension of the host's style and taste, complete with personal touches—family photographs, a bookcase filled with favorite decorative objects and books—anything that helps create a homey environment at the same time that it gives guests a place to retreat to. (Which can sometimes be as much a relief for the hostess as it is for the guest).

Within the bounds of space and budget, the weekend host should attempt to provide everything that she would want as a guest, a pampered guest. But the true pampering comes in anticipating any necessities that might have been forgotten.

Aside from some quiet, private space, a guest bedroom and bath should include the obvious—a comfortable bed; soft BIG towels; plenty of sturdy hangers; good lighting; strong hair dryer and a supply of toilet paper.

Note: Avoid the obvious pitfalls—treating this spare space as a collection of unwanted furniture and cramming the closets and drawers full of cast-offs.

Following is a thorough checklist of almost any and everything a houseguest could require:

Bedroom Accoutrements

- twin beds (one hard, one soft)
- two pillows per guest (one down, one firm)
- ample supply of blankets or a down quilt
- Itty Bitty Booklite for reading in bed when all lights are off
- bedside clock-radio with alarm
- sufficient good quality hangers—sturdy wooden pant and suit; padded satin; practical plastic
- bureau drawer lined with lightly-scented paper

- bedside carafe with water glass
- eyeshade
- sewing kit with scissors
- books and magazines
- phone with silence switch
- scented candle
- clothes brush
- dimestore reading glasses
- note pads and pencil
- full-length mirror (at the back of closet, if space doesn't permit in the room)
- iron and ironing board in a location convenient to guest room

SHORT SUBJECT

"Sleeping Around"
Emily Post suggests . . .

Sleep in your own guest room every now and then, to keep a close watch on details:
- ▲ Are the drawers cluttered with odds and ends?
- ▲ Do you need another plug for the hair dryer?
- ▲ Is the bed getting lumpy or beginning to smell musty?
- ▲ Is the shower curtain rod about to come unscrewed?
- ▲ Is the most recent magazine dated 1962?
- ▲ Are mosquitoes sneaking through the torn screen?
- ▲ Does the room feel stuffy at night—or is there a strong draft coming through the hard-to-close window?
- ▲ Are smells from the kitchen coming up through the heating outlets?

Bathroom Amenities

- two full sets of towels (bath, hand, wash, bath mat)
- special soaps/bubble bath/bath oil/loofah/bath salts
- shampoo/conditioner
- facial tissue
- supply of toilet paper
- hair dryer and brushes/comb
- small pack of makeup brushes
- perfumes/aftershave
- night light
- plumber's friend
- wastebasket

Medicine cabinet:
- nail brush and pumice
- new toothbrush and tooth paste
- disposable razor
- Alka-seltzer/aspirin
- first aid kit

- mouth wash
- feminine hygiene necessities
- cotton balls and Q-tips
- suntan block
- sunburn lotion
- Evian atomizer
- insect repellent

Manicure essentials:
- polish remover
- emery board
- glaze
- hand cream

And for the guest bath that also serves as a "powder room"
- linen or terry, perhaps paper, hand towels
- special soaps
- scented candle
- flowers
- perfume
- decorative comb and brush
- room spray

The condition of guest bath amenities should not look like a resting place for your leftover cosmetics, nor should it resemble a hotel's room samples to take home. Happy medium? "Homey" essentials for a guest's convenience while in your home.

Use clear plastic bottles with specific labels (shampoo, conditioner, hand cream). This "generic" approach makes it easy for you to refill after the weekend so that the next guest doesn't have to face half-used bottles of this and that.

A note regarding proper sound insulation—
A guest room is a place to escape to. It loses this function when guests must continue on "best behavior" because they are overhearing private conversations—and rightfully assume that theirs can be overheard as well. Insufficient soundproofing also subjects guests to kitchen bangings, babies crying, a teenager's rock music.

And for those would-be chatelaines . . . some final elegant and extravagant tips for your chateau's guest room and bath:

- ꙮ separate lounging and reading area

- ꙮ television in guest room

- ꙮ private bar, completely stocked, to include great "munchies"

- ꙮ new magazines selected with guest's specific interests in mind

- ꙮ heated towel rack

- ꙮ fresh bottled water by bedside each day

- ꙮ luxurious linens

- ꙮ the bed made daily, turned down at night

- ꙮ private telephone line

- ꙮ newspaper outside the door for early risers

- ꙮ phone intercom linked to kitchen

- ꙮ maid who can press linens and cottons and repair any clothes

- ꙮ dressing table and makeup mirror

- ꙮ makeup kit for the ladies

- ꙮ chocolates and mints, re-filled daily

- ꙮ bowl of fruit

- ꙮ luxurious terry cloth robes

- ꙮ private stock of beach or exercise towels

- ꙮ masseuse on-call

- ꙮ jacuzzi

- ꙮ new set of towels daily

- ꙮ breakfast in bed

Overseen and Overheard

Pet Peeves of the Host

Guests who . . .

✦ leave dishes around, or in the sink, without putting them in the dishwasher.

✦ want to take over.

✦ won't leave in a timely fashion after the party is over.

✦ use all the hot water for a shower.

✦ arrive overburdened with large suitcases.

✦ use bathroom towels for the beach and then forget them.

✦ assume that you are going to take them to or go with them on *every* outing.

✦ are too casual about the use of a septic tank.

✦ disregard droughts, water shortages and private wells.

✦ reorganize kitchen cabinets, rearrange the guest room.

✦ expect to be the constant center of attention.

✦ leave the Sunday paper strewn all over.

✦ "use" the host only as a bed or way to "get there" and then spend a majority of their time running around to all the social events they can engineer.

✦ appear at times that compromise your generosity and ability to decline (i.e., after the last ferry has left).

✦ "plop," expecting to be waited on, entertained, provided for 24 hours a day.

✦ are impolite to servants or other guests.

✦ are improperly attired, despite specifics being provided about weekend activities.

✦ must borrow everything.

✦ run up the phone bill.

Pet Peeves of the Guest

Hosts who . . .

◇ invite too many people, so that the weekend seems more like a three-ring circus than an enjoyable visit.

◇ over-plan, over-schedule, over-program.

◇ serve too much, too rich food.

◇ leave you on your own for breakfast without instructions for the exotic coffee maker.

◇ run out of hot water for showers.

◇ offer soft, lumpy, sagging beds.

◇ provide only cast-off, twisted, rusted wire clothes hangers.

◇ require guests to *work* for a party.

◇ entertain to impress, not through genuine pleasure in spending time with friends.

◇ let the family dog, with fleas, sleep on your bed.

◇ don't provide enough towels, or provide only a few threadbare ones.

◇ are so disorganized they run out of ice during a cocktail party or can't get dinner ready before 10:45 p.m.

◇ call guests just before they are to leave for the week-end with a list of "to brings."

◇ provide no privacy or "escape" place.

◇ make the guest feel guilty for wanting to read or nap.

◇ don't stock enough food in the fridge, so guests *have* to go grocery shopping.

◇ plan for majority of meals to be taken in restaurants then don't offer to pick up their share of the bill.

How to Get Invited Back

Weekend visits and hostess gifts go hand-in-hand. And while you may choose, correctly, to send a real gift after the visit, you should plan to arrive with something *in hand*—be it a bunch of daisies or a European decorating magazine.

The following pages enumerate the many choices, selections and ideas for gifting the weekend host or hostess. But the first principle of giving is that the object of appreciation be *thoughtful*—in other words, given a lot of thought for and about the host. After all, hosts are doing you a favor by having you in their home—feeding you, sheltering you, providing entertainment.

Something that you've enjoyed and use daily says something very personal. It will give the host a chance to think of "you using yours while they're using theirs."

Another vote for hostess gifts comes under the "win-her-gratitude-with-your-sharp-eye-for-details" award. This shows that you truly put a lot of thought into your gift by keeping those eyes and ears open.

For example:

Did you linger over coffee and conversation at the breakfast table? Then consider covered mugs with deep saucers for keeping coffee hot longer. They are practical and attractive all on their own once other plates are removed.

Would a necessary amenity for the guest bath be received as a big favor? Pamper her with a terry-covered tub headrest for those afternoon baths that she so enjoys.

Did you hear her complain about x, y or z? There's your clue for what to send with your thanks.

Was fresh squeezed orange juice a treat you enjoyed each morning? Pamper her with a marvelous crystal or ceramic pitcher or appeal to her practical side with a square glass juice jug which utilizes refrigerator space efficiently and is handsome enough to put on the breakfast table.

Were mosquitoes a problem when dining outdoors? Consider small metal cones, filled with citronella wax, on spikes to stick into herb pots, flower arrangements, garden edging.

Hostess Gifts and House Presents

Often it's easier to come up with a gift if you think in specific categories. So the following hostess gift and house present suggestions approach gift-giving from many different angles. One thing to keep in mind—personalizing a gift, with the host's name or initials, adds immeasurably to the intrinsic value of your offering. Many objects, from an oversized tin of popcorn to a telephone note pad, can be ordered with this simple, yet very effective addition.

As a sure bet, consider a photographic essay of the weekend, in its own personalized album, as a sure bet for pleasing that weekend host or hostess.

Witty and Whimsical Gifts
The extravagance comes in the creativity, not the price.

- mini-sized legal pads, for note taking or correspondence, boasting a witty headline (i.e., Re-partee from Pardee)

- the weekend house, cut out of wood and handpainted, as a Christmas ornament

- a sponge-painted flower pot, showing off your artistic talents, packed with fresh flowers

- monogrammed cardboard coasters

- personalized cookie jar

- snapshot puzzle—a favorite picture from the weekend turned into a puzzle with 150 or 494 pieces

- reproduction of an antique "Bed and Breakfast" sign personalized with the hostess's name

- jumbo tin of popcorn, emblazoned with a phrase reminiscent of a funny happenstance

- a rainbow's worth of paper cocktail napkins, printed with a weekend appropriate phrase ("Whad' ya expect, linen?")

For the Entertaining Host or Hostess

- set of six mother-of-pearl paté spreaders

- set of mint leaf patterned iced tea spoons

- beeswax candles or unusually-styled tapers

- porcelain rendition of a circular Camembert box, with underplate, for serving and storing cheese

- steel mesh food cover for outdoor buffets—to keep unwanted airborne guests away

- portable polystyrene combination cooler/beach chair

- large beach mat with woven backgammon or checkers board

- woven slat wood ice bucket that's strong enough to use as an extra seat

- an anthology of rock and roll radio, 1955-1964, complete with actual deejay patter and original commercials

- flip-through CD rack

- set of oversized 13-inch buffet plates

- drinks pitcher for Bloody Marys, etc.

- 12-inch long blown glass swizzle sticks

- powdered sugar shaker (for summer strawberries, breakfast waffles, French toast)

- fruit forks and knives

- antique lobster forks and picks

- small pitcher specifically for syrup

Necessities for the House

- personalized, telephone-side note pads

- mini, clip-on flashlight with flexible neck

- quilt or comforter rack

- painted bed tray

- small basket just the right size for breakfast jams

- breakfast juice glasses

- hot air popcorn popper

- boot scrape

- water conserving shower head

- special antique furniture oils or wax repair sticks

- plastic pitcher with replaceable filter that removes metals and chlorine taste

- mini countertop toaster oven

- surge protector for audio/video plug-ins

- videocassette "eraser" for removing noise from re-recorded tapes

PARDEE TIP

One hostess implores . . .
"Keep the presents small. All our houses are over-decorated."

NOTE:

Most second homes are fairly new (not passed down from family to family) and so practical gifts are not only appreciated but are kind to the hostess's pocketbook and to-do list.

Finds for the Gourmet

- collection of spice and oil essentials—(avocado oil, raspberry vinaigrette, bourbon vanilla beans)

- metal olive oil jugs with non-drip plastic spout

- casual decanters—much more attractive than wine bottles—and originally intended for other pur-poses. Recruit glass containers, flower vases, martini pitchers, water carafes, even chemical beakers

- pitchers—you can never have enough to use for breakfast orange juice, brunch Bloody Marys, afternoon sangrias

- collection of mini herb pots, with their own tray, for the kitchen window

- ship in some live Maine lobsters, packed into a cooking pot, with moist seaweed and a reusable ice pack. To include, of course, two pot holders and a supply of shell-crackers, picks, bibs and place mats.

- All the fixings for a Cajun Crawfish Boil, shipped in —12 pounds live crawfish, 20 quart boiling pot, Cajun seasonings, fail-proof instructions

- Seven pounds of jumbo green asparagus, shipped May to July

PARDEE TIP

To come bearing a cookbook is to bring a peace offering in the face of a hostess's trepidations . . . to come laden with all the foodstuffs and ingredients will endear you forever.

Gifts for the Gardener

- a rare bulb

- wildflower seeds computer-selected to suit the host's specific soil and climate

- an herbal topiary

- indoor bulbs with their own container inspired by the decor of the weekend retreat

- decorative painted watering can with the hostess's name or initials

- garden statuary

- a guest's favorite, hard-to-find, pruning shears

- tole cachepots

- blue and white Chinese porcelain wall planter

- a crushable, foldable straw gardening hat

- 100 daffodil bulbs

- stone gate post balls

- terra cotta garden edgings

- goatskin gardening gloves

Perfect Pamper Presents

So-called because they are an indulgence—something a hostess wouldn't usually buy for herself—but they please through their femininity, beauty and detail. A great part of their success comes from the careful attention given to the packaging and presentation.

- scented drawer liner paper

- mohair sofa throw

- heart-shaped cedar block tied in cutwork linen and hanging from a silken cord

- floral drawer organizers

- set of four embroidered cotton guest towels nested in a lace-trimmed fabric box

- hard-to-find ingredients for romantic champagne drinks—peach puree for Bellinis, raspberry puree carnevale

- potpourri tied in the finest mesh gold tulle

- silverhandled makeup brushes

. . . And pamper presents, gathered into pretty baskets or other inspired containers, make "perfectly pleasing house gifts". Remember—it's the originality, not the contents, that counts.

Weekend Brunch Basket
A brilliant-colored straw bag, with double leather shoulder straps, serves up the accoutrements for thoughtful entertaining—personalized cocktail napkins, secret family recipe Bloody Mary mix, pitcher, chintz-covered hangers for the guest coat closet, two specially recorded music cassettes—and then becomes a summer tote for the hostess.

M'lady's Basket
A hand painted straw basket filled with fragrances, drawer sachets, miniature boudoir pillow with embroidered case, needlepointed "do not disturb" door sign and a night shirt.

Cookie Lover's Basket
Wire mesh apple picker's basket, lined with a pastry cloth, holds a personalized cookie jar and cookie cutters, framed handwritten favorite recipes, gold and silver paper muffin cups, cookie decorating accessories, pastry brush.

Garden Bounty Basket
A woven market basket offering up a selection of seasonal vegetables that "travel well"—asparagus, artichokes, Belgian endive, colored peppers, radicchio—plus pasta, fresh potted herbs and spices.

Bathing Beauty Basket
A plastic-lined, ribbon-decorated basket stuffed with everything for the bath—scented soaps, bubble bath, natural sponges, bath oils and salts, an inflatable pillow for the tub—to then become a creative wastebasket for the bathroom.

Tisket, Tasket Tea Basket
An English "trug" garden basket, lined with an old embroidered linen tea cloth, is packed with a small painted tin tea tray, jar of double Devon cream, scone mix, homemade strawberry jam, tea strainer and stand, three small tins of tea, amber rock crystal sugar—and an antique cup and saucer.

And for the Host Who Has Everything . . .

♠ a good photo of the weekend retreat turned into postcards

♠ chocolate mushrooms in a handcrafted wooden crate

♠ eighteen flavors of jelly beans in a lucite "tackle box"

♠ battery-operated computer

♠ heated towel bar

♠ guaranteed jet lag diet

♠ self-soaping back sponge

♠ special seeds or cuttings from the guest's own regional garden

♠ a clothes lint electric shaver

♠ brass engraved ID tag, à la hotels, for extra set of house keys. Guests can "drop in any mailbox" if they accidentally walk off with them

♠ needlepoint pillow kit of fish that says: "You still here?"

♠ unique china collectibles: i.e., antique majolica cheese keeps

♠ a set of hand-painted (ideally by guest) botanicals depicting the hostess's favorites from her garden

---

S H O R T   S U B J E C T

An alternative to an object as a gift? A much-appreciated gesture on the part of a guest is to "treat" the assembled weekenders to a specific activity—a midnight catamaran sail, trap shooting session, hot air balloon rides. Much appreciated, too, because the host has also been given an assist in entertaining the guests.

+ silverplated toothbrush and razor

+ a painted wooden fire screen detailing the family tree of the host's favorite dog

+ a 10 magnitude star (visible with a telescope) named for the host, then filed in the International Star Registry vaults in Switzerland

+ a computerized mattress that fills with air to compensate automatically for a partner's movements

+ develop a rose specifically hybridized for and named after the hostess (through the American Rose Society in Shreveport, LA)

+ gouache rendering of the hostess's favorite weekend room or any other interior of her retreat

+ a crossword puzzle designed specifically around the host's life experiences

+ silver-handled ice cream scoop

The "We Love Them, But . . ." Awards
OR *Diary of a Wrung-out Weekend Participant*

A collection of amusing—after the fact—tales and anecdotes that have been encountered by those who entertain and are entertained on the weekends.

▼ The talented but riotous artist who drops the large economy-size bottle of olive oil in the middle of the kitchen tile floor as you're dishing up dinner for sixteen.

▼ The well-meaning houseguest who pops all the various colored sheets into the washing machine—along with her husband's new red bandana.

▼ The professionally proficient but socially handicapped lawyer who presents her hostess with a detailed list of will-do's and wont-do's, to include the time of her afternoon nap and her favorite teas.

▼ The scatterbrained lady of the house who plans a weekend of elegant festivities but overlooks the broken plumbing—and blithely waves her guests to the neighbor's facilities next door.

▼ The invited guest who arrives with an uninvited German shepherd named Ladybug, who proceeds to scratch the paint off the dining room windowsills.

▼ The well-traveled guest who leaves his shoes outside his bedroom door, forgetting that he is in a humble cottage and not in a four-star hotel.

▼ The insomniac guest who decides to rearrange your entire downstairs at 3:00 a.m. before taking the 7:10 train back to the city.

> *"A good holiday is one spent among people whose notions of time are vaguer than yours."*
> —J. B. Priestley

GREAT WEEKEND ENTERTAINING

II

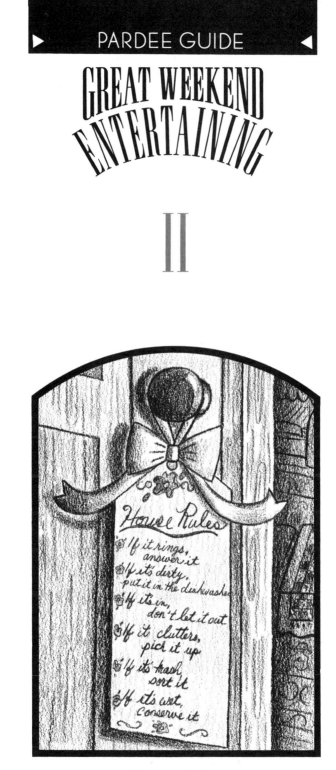

Essential
WEEKEND LOGISTICS

ESSENTIAL WEEKEND LOGISTICS

Notes on Keeping House

Taking Stock

Weekend retreats become great getaway spots when both house and host convey an air of ease. And as many a wise hostess has learned, the luxury of leisure comes with careful planning.

Leaving your troubles behind—and enjoying that leisure—is what weekends are all about. How to ensure that weekday troubles do not creep into weekend time? Become good friends with the save-your-sanity duo, **planning** and **organization**. Start by taking note of the following practical and creative suggestions for trouble-proofing your weekend.

▲ Since clutter seems to be a given of human nature . . . Establish one central place to which every family member's "treasures" can be relegated. This way you won't be left struggling with odds and ends clean-up as houseguests are pulling *into* the driveway—or you are pulling *out* of the driveway to go home. It is up to each individual to rescue his or her belongings.

▲ So many weekend summer places enjoy the glory of bright sunshine, but it can be a mixed blessing if you're trying to sleep late. Consider interlining draperies with "blackout" fabric or hanging a separate blackout shade.

▲ Schedule guests, or otherwise carve out time for yourself, to wind down and close the house at the end of the weekend— shut and bolt windows, empty trash, turn on dishwasher, organize "take home" paraphernalia.

▲ Weekends are not supposed to be about cleaning, but if you have no choice, at least make it as painless as possible. Pick up one of the many books available on speed cleaning and promise yourself that you will perfect the art of the "20-minute clean house schedule."

△ When leaving after the weekend, add one cup of chlorine bleach to toilet bowls; this reduces water rings.

△ Silence noisy floor boards by sprinkling a little talcum powder into the cracks.

△ Plump and air down pillows by running them through the clothes dryer for 30 minutes.

Appliances, Plus

Don't set foot in your weekend haven unless you have as many time-saving gadgets as your budget will permit. Delegating to state-of-the-art electronic wonders can *give you back* many hours that would otherwise be lost in a day. Some suggestions:

Food Processor
Use it; don't be concerned with the bit of clean up it requires.

Cordless Vacuum Cleaner
◆ It's *convenient*. Always charged, can be wall-mounted to conserve space, eliminating the need to drag out a cumbersome vacuum cleaner.

◆ It's *versatile*. Works on both dry *and* wet spills.

◆ It's *neat*. Lets you clean up unobtrusively and then empties in seconds.

Dishwasher
Invest wisely; at the least, the middle choice in the mid-price bracket. Consider the "entertaining whiz" options:
◆ adjustable upper rack for either tall glasses on top or large serving dishes below; tilt capacity also

◆ "flash dry" capability—no waiting around for dishes to dry

◆ up to nine-hour delay option (so dishwasher can be set to start automatically after everyone's asleep)

Percolator or Computerized Coffee Maker
Makes for one less project to be concerned with while trying to fix breakfast or dinner for many guests.

Quick Decorating Details

With many weekend retreats, the coziness that we love translates into the space that we lack. Short of costly add-ons or major rearranging, there are other ways to seek that space that may be hiding from you. A treasure hunt for under-utilized or overlooked spots will usually point up the fact that the space you crave may already exist.

Skirting the issue
Over a table, under a sink, around a bed—for the sake of economy, nothing delivers more space for less investment than a skirt. On a volume basis, the space under a skirted table is the equivalent of another chest of drawers or small closet.

Window workout
Bring charm and romance into your weekend getaway, plus storage—create a window seat enclosed on either side by closets *or* hinge the tops of a banquette in a bay window alcove.

Hall, yes
On a volume basis, halls take up more space and contribute less than any spot in your home. So . . .

◇ Build in shallow shelves to showcase collectibles, photographs, etc.

◇ Hang decorative baskets in groupings that are accessible for storage.

◇ Brighten a hallway with pattern-covered boxes placed on shelf brackets interspersed in an eye-pleasing arrangement.

And don't forget
In any room . . .

☛ long shelves that are placed high, near the ceiling, up and out of the way

☛ baskets that are hung from a kitchen ceiling or pan rack

☛ a hinged trunk styled as an ottoman seat

Practicalities

Don't labor under the misconception that sheets belong only in a bedroom—introduce them to the rest of the house and see what a dividend they can be. Not only do they give you the opportunity to change a decorating scheme instantly, and cost effectively, but some of these old tricks help make a place cozier.

- Drape sheets and linens over dreary upholstery, gathering them into place with cording or ribbon.

- Cut tablecloths (up to 48" diameter tables) from flat sheets: add a smaller square overlay in a different pattern.

- Transform a small room by stapling sheets to all four walls.

- Skirt a bathroom sink.

- Cover cushions with printed pillowcases.

- Make a decorative garden parasol or create a folding screen from a favorite "designer sheet."

- Change the look of a window with a simple stationary balloon pouf.

- Create an alcove with draped sheeting.

S HORT SUBJECT

"Hot Issue"

Running out of hot water made the Top Ten list for pet peeves—on both guest's and host's part. The following brilliant but simple solution can eliminate this annoyance that always seems to come with weekend entertaining.

Outfit your guest bathroom with its own under-counter electric water heater. Operated independently from the main heater, it can be installed with an on-off switch, thereby keeping your electric bill trimmed when not in use. And the compact 20-30 gallon tank will provide enough hot water for two quick showers when turned on two to three hours before guests arrive.

Closing and Opening the Weekend House for the Season

The following draw upon many different weekend living circumstances and house needs. Using these as a memory jogger, make a list of each task required in your *own* seasonal ritual, assigning the amount of time each takes.

Closing

❏ Pull shades.

❏ Take curtains down and roll up rugs to guard against fading.

❏ Cover upholstered furniture.

❏ Move dark wood furniture out of direct sun.

❏ Put blankets in moth balls.

❏ Throw out old food.

❏ Set out mouse pellets.

❏ Wrap packaged foods in plastic to mouse- and ant-proof.

❏ Put up exterior plywood covers over sliding glass doors.

❏ Pump and drain water heater.

❏ Drain all water out of house.

❏ Shut down all utilities except those required for emergency purposes.

❏ Have plumber put anti-freeze in toilet, washing machine, dishwasher.

❏ Take down screens; put up storm shutters.

Special precautions:

❏ Hide silver, liquor, TV and stereo (so as not to tempt thieves).

❏ Establish one lockable room or closet (and don't forget where you hide the key).

❏ Leave heat set to 45 degrees to keep walls warm and avoid cracked plaster.

❏ **Don't forget to take out the garbage.**

Opening

- ❑ Perform thorough house cleaning.

- ❑ Rotate curtains when hanging.

- ❑ Fill hot water tank.

- ❑ Take off slipcovers.

- ❑ Service outboard motors, lawnmower.

- ❑ Oil fishing rods, gardening tools.

- ❑ Take gardening pots, wintered plants out of storage.

- ❑ Move clothes.

- ❑ Take cars out of storage, and have serviced.

- ❑ Put out porch furniture.

Don't Forget:

- ❑ Send change of address to magazines, newspapers.

- ❑ Fold outs that haven't been aired out.

P A R D E E   T I P

To keep new batteries "everlasting," store them in a
moisture-free zip-lock plastic bag in the refrigerator.

Appliances: "Closed for the Season"

Few things are more frustrating than facing a new season with a list of costly and inconvenient clean-ups—and appliances that greet you in mixed states of breakdown. Both can be avoided if you observe a few quick precautions.

Water-using appliances:

1. Trip circuit breaker.
2. Shut off water supply to unit.
3. Proceed to remove water in inlet or outlet pipes.

Dishwasher
❏ Remove lower access panel below door.

❏ Using a crescent wrench, disconnect water line that comes up from the floor and let water flow out.

❏ Pull off water inlet valve and blow into it to dislodge any remaining water (this assures that there will only be air in the pipes).

❏ Reattach inlet valve and hose to machine.

❏ Remove "sump" cover under machine and sponge up water in rubber boot.

❏ Replace old water with one-half cup white vinegar in rubber boot (vinegar keeps pump seals from drying out; it also has a low freezing point).

❏ Replace "sump" cover.

Refrigerator
❏ Disconnect water line where it connects to refrigerator.

❏ Empty ice tray and let icemaker go through a complete cycle, thereby flushing out small amount of water remaining in water line.

❏ Unplug refrigerator.

- [ ] Clean interior with baking soda and disinfectant (a main priority).

- [ ] Leave both refrigerator and freezer door slightly ajar, placing a wedge under doors so they won't sag.

Washing machine
- [ ] Using crescent wrench, remove hoses from back of machine.

- [ ] Remove back panel.

- [ ] With wrench, remove two interior hoses where they meet pump.

- [ ] Drain hoses, catching the water in a bucket.

- [ ] Plug in machine and turn on wash cycle for a few seconds to flush any water out of the pump.

- [ ] Reattach pump hoses; replace back cover.

- [ ] **Do not hook up water lines til next year.**

Electrical appliances

- [ ] Disconnect or unplug all units.

- [ ] Keep them moisture-free by wrapping in towels or paper and then covering completely with plastic.

Gas appliances

- [ ] Turn off gas valve.

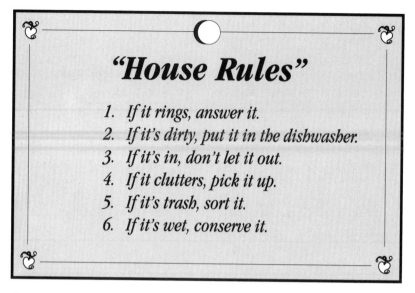

"House Rules"

1. *If it rings, answer it.*
2. *If it's dirty, put it in the dishwasher.*
3. *If it's in, don't let it out.*
4. *If it clutters, pick it up.*
5. *If it's trash, sort it.*
6. *If it's wet, conserve it.*

An artistic and effective way to communicate your personal preferences—hand-lettered and drawn, in a pretty frame hanging from a ribbon.

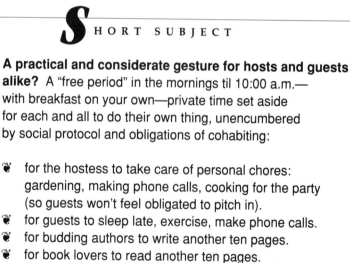

S HORT SUBJECT

A practical and considerate gesture for hosts and guests alike? A "free period" in the mornings til 10:00 a.m.—with breakfast on your own—private time set aside for each and all to do their own thing, unencumbered by social protocol and obligations of cohabiting:

- for the hostess to take care of personal chores: gardening, making phone calls, cooking for the party (so guests won't feel obligated to pitch in).
- for guests to sleep late, exercise, make phone calls.
- for budding authors to write another ten pages.
- for book lovers to read another ten pages.
- for the jock to run or take an early morning cliff walk.
- for golfers and fishermen to depart early . . . guiltless.
- for children to . . .

Breakfast Note: Ask ahead to see what guests like in the morning. Having a well-stocked larder makes it easier on everyone, especially if guests are expected to fend for themselves at breakfast time.

Food and Drink

Relaxed, renewing, uncomplicated—the same tempo that we expect of our weekend—should apply to food preparation as well. This means: simple menus, brief recipes, readily available ingredients and making a play on the fresh and seasonal. Weekend cookery should be either very quick, a tasteful meal turned out in a half-hour, or very slow, put on before you venture out for the day.

Other useful observations:
K.I.S.S. (Keep It Simple, Silly)—A weekend host's mantra.
The following useful observations are all variations on this theme.

1. Be Realistic.
Understand that you can't be a servant and host at the same time.

♦ Know how long each dish takes to prepare and what should be done when (i.e., marinating the meat overnight, starting the grill early evening).

♦ Tell guests what you want them to bring and don't be embarrassed about it (they're going to bring something anyway, so it might as well dovetail with your menu plans).

♦ Tell yourself that you're only going to allocate _x_ amount of time to cooking and preparation—and stick to it!

2. Avoid "Death by Cooking."

Summer entertaining fare should not be taken too seriously. This is the time and place for family favorites and old standbys—homemade butterscotch sauce, seafood stew from the daily catch, grandmother's famous peach ice cream. *PLUS*

◇ In the summer, let nature design the menu. Play on the fruits and vegetables of the season. Add meat or fish on the grill and you've caught the spirit of summer.

◇ In the winter, cozy up to creative casseroles or appetite-pleasing one-dish meals.

3. Be Creative.

◇ Go for expandable menus. During "high-season" one invitation can result in six people appearing.

◇ Go for interchangeable dishes. Recipes should act as "culinary coordinates," able to be mixed and matched over the span of the weekend.

◇ Go for recycling. Friday night's hot grilled vegetables can serve double-duty in pasta salad for Sunday's lunch.

4. Work smart, not hard.

◇ Experience the "thrill of the grill"—and kiss the kitchen goodbye. Everything but dessert can be produced on this efficient American mainstay—from grilled vegetables to smoked corn to barbecued chicken.

◇ Spare yourself from hot weather cooking—and guests from appetite-suppressing heat—by serving cold foods.

◇ Become a devotee of "take-away" resources. Time saved on cooking goes into festive and eye-catching presentations.

◇ Or cook everything ahead and bring out with you.

◇ Count on drinks that can be mixed and served in a big pitcher (margaritas, sangria, martinis, daiquiris). All the better if they can be pre-cooled, dispensing with the need for melting ice cubes.

Short Orders

♦ Plan accordingly, so you don't run out of food or liquor on Sunday (either can be logistically difficult to procure given blue laws or lackadaisical habits of local resources).

♦ Have a well-stocked freezer and pantry, so you aren't caught empty-handed.

♦ Develop a set of menus with which you are thoroughly familiar and comfortable, transferring all recipes to index cards that are at home in their own file box. Then laminate the recipe cards so they can stand up to dampness, greasy fingers, spills and well-intentioned guests.

♦ Plan menus to include specific "to do" notes so that if you choose to apportion tasks, they will already be spelled out.

Indulge in cookery pieces and accessories that will create a conversation piece and be part of the fun of helping:

◊ a Crogue Monsieur toasting iron to make shell-shaped grilled sandwiches for LUNCH

◊ deep black metal paella pan for one large Dutch apple "pancake" at BREAKFAST

◊ an ice shaver for tropical drinks.

◊ *Or* . . . make every meal a variation on a picnic or box lunch.

SHORT SUBJECT

The first meal after guests arrive should be casual, ideally a buffet for flexibility and "easing in."

PLUS
Of buffets: In addition to budget and mobility—
Guests can move about, meeting other guests at their pace, not getting locked into one spot or one group. They have more choices of conversation partners, food offerings.
Hosts can expand or reduce, move indoors or out, add or take away dishes.

PICNICS: *Feasting Alfresco*

Is it true that food eaten outdoors always seems to taste better? Or is it the romance and change of locale that we yearn for in our weekends?

Whatever the case, many hosts share a bit of conventional wisdom about picnics that concludes—if you can't do it right, don't do it at all. Worse than pesky ants are plastic forks that break, styrofoam plates that wobble, containers that leak.

Part of the fun of picnicing is assembling all the accoutrements for a tailor-made basket or hamper that suits your entertaining needs. And opting for quality in your selection of staples— stainless flatware, heavy duty plastic plates and glasses—means that you will always be prepared to move the dining experience outside—in style. Or, transfer it just as easily inside for a refreshing twist on the typical.

Keep this idea in mind, for a well-executed indoor "picnic" offers an offbeat and creative dining option that makes for high-spirited occasions . . . and relaxed guests—as though in being unorthodox yourself you have sanctioned it for them.

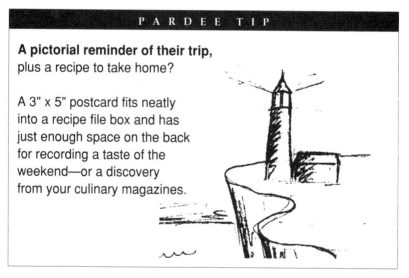

P A R D E E   T I P

A pictorial reminder of their trip, plus a recipe to take home?

A 3" x 5" postcard fits neatly into a recipe file box and has just enough space on the back for recording a taste of the weekend—or a discovery from your culinary magazines.

"The best you can offer your guests is the unexpected."

—Elsa Maxwell

Tips for dining in the great outdoors:

* Start with a written check-list specifically suiting the menu, the terrain and the number of guests.

* If foods are going to go un-refrigerated or be out in the sun for a while, avoid mayonnaise and dairy product bases.

* Stackable, tight-sealing containers not only help you efficiently organize a small space but ensure that you won't be dealing with messy leaks.

* Don't forget special ther-moses to keep your hot and cold liquids at the proper temperatures.

* Always include a ground cloth—not only does it keep posteriors from get-ting damp or dusty, it also offers a decorative element while defining the "dining area."

* Be as creative with this environment as you would with your dining table back home—mix colors, textures, paper, linen; yes, even plastic plates with ceramic dishes.

* For impromptu dining alfresco? Keep a grill top in your car trunk (you can always find wood); news-paper is a great insulator, keeping frozen things cold and serving a second use as kindling for fire.

* *Box* meals are the ultimate picnic luxury—nothing to cook, no empty hamper to lug back home, no dishes to wash.

P A R D E E   T I P

Press napkin rings into service to band together flatware and napkins for easy travel.

Necessities to pop into your picnic basket.

Pack the following in their own container that is ready at all times to act as your "emergency kit":

* corkscrew/bottle opener
* sunscreen
* small garbage bag
* matches

* salt and pepper
* knife, large spoon
* wet wipes
* adhesive bandages

Weekend Troubleshooters

❖ Make sure you have an ample supply of dishes and dining staples (i.e., coffee mugs) so you don't have to run the dishwasher three times a day to keep up with demand.

❖ Be thoughtful when considering silver-plated flatware (tempting, when it's the same price as stainless or on sale "for a bargain")—most of it *does not* wear well in the dishwasher.

❖ Invest in the best quality terry bath towels you can afford. You'll need something that can stand up to all the washing and wear they'll get.

❖ Type up, or hand-letter, kitchen "love notes" so guests venturing into the kitchen alone or at odd hours will know how

to turn on the temperamental disposal, how to work the "state of the art" coffee grinder, where to find the _____.

Put up, or leave in guest's room, other "love notes" relating to turning off outside lights (if coming home later than host), turning on security system, leaving animals in or out, house idiosyncracies. It also saves the host from having to remember to think of *everything*.

❖ Tired of receiving misinformation about flight arrivals and waiting hours at the airport for arriving guests? Note the direct line phone numbers of the airline counters at your local airport (not to be confused with the published airline numbers for arrivals and departures). This will ensure you more personal service and current information (i.e., the plane hasn't left the ground in _____. Unless a plane is already airborne, the flight information is not current.).

❖ In some weekend households, with a mix of age groups and interests, comings and goings may take place well into the night. As a courtesy, *and* security measure, install motion detector lighting for both outdoors and indoors. This eliminates the issue of "last one in, turn off the lights," while ensuring the host that the important areas inside and outside will always be lit when houseguests arrive home.

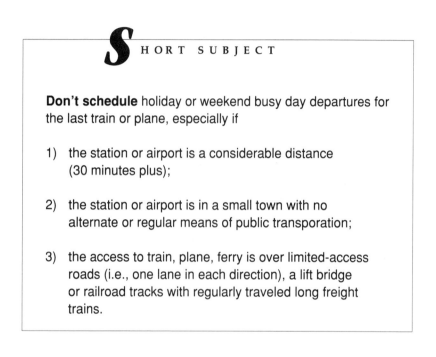

S H O R T   S U B J E C T

Don't schedule holiday or weekend busy day departures for the last train or plane, especially if

1) the station or airport is a considerable distance (30 minutes plus);

2) the station or airport is in a small town with no alternate or regular means of public transporation;

3) the access to train, plane, ferry is over limited-access roads (i.e., one lane in each direction), a lift bridge or railroad tracks with regularly traveled long freight trains.

In Praise of Practicalities

One of the great tenets of weekend entertaining? Stay flexible: parties can multiply as one invitation results in a friend, plus their two, four or six houseguests; the weather can turn on you, prompting an immediate lurch to contingency plans.

◆ **Ask in advance what guests would specifically like to do** when they visit you. Not only does this give you a feeling for the anticipated tempo of the weekend, but the answers can be provocative (i.e., "I'm going to Africa to see the gorillas at 9,000 feet and I need to walk two hours a day to get in shape"). Often guests will have read an article in some far-flung publication or local paper providing insight on your town that may be news to you. Houseguests also give you the opportunity to look at your environs and scheduled activities from a fresh perspective.

◆ **Hear, hear! for outdoor cooking—and eating!** Serving lunch outside in baskets or boxes not only saves dishwashing but also leaves the kitchen clean and free for dinner activity.

◆ **Call your local Tupperware representative.** Even if you don't want to have one of those vintage '60s "Tupperware parties," you should become familiar with this resource. They were the first to make freezer proof, airtight solid plastic containers. And, in the process, Tupperware has become a past master at organization, designing stackable, easily portable, efficient food storage containers—everything from pie carriers to cracker boxes.

---

*S*HORT SUBJECT

Need a creative and romantic alternative to a "traditional" guest room? Consider an elegant, screened-in tent, large enough for standing and moving about in, and decorated to include hanging pictures. Include a seating area and dressing table outside, under a canopy, to enhance the illusion of roughing it—in style. Pitch this tent-guest room where it is shaded by day and protected from strong breezes at night.

BE PREPARED!

❏ A typed list of "to-do's" within a one-hour radius *even if you don't hand it out,* is a memory jogger for you when you're being pulled in three directions.

❏ Updated "restaurant review" with your comments regarding dress code.

❏ Must-haves:
- *current* commuter plane, train, ferry schedules
- detailed map to house and map of area
- idiosyncracies of local natives, terrain, authorities, animals
- placards or signposts to put out for arriving houseguests, or before a party if your location is hard to find
- a rolodex or business card file noting all local resources, including business hours and any special information (i.e., owner's home phone number).

In the Marketplace:

Many hostesses feel that "a house is not a home without flowers." So, for transporting long-stemmed beauties from your weekend gardening spot to your city home—or bringing flora with you to greet arriving weekend guests—consider the easily portable Bloomsaver—three heavy duty plastic containers fused together and fitted with a 16-inch-long lexon handle. Not only can you keep flowers fresh in water while cutting them but the well-balanced and stable design affords great travel-ability.

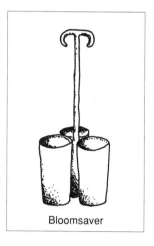

Bloomsaver

GREAT WEEKEND ENTERTAINING

III

SOCIAL CIRCUMSTANCES

Social
Circumstances

Common Courtesies

From kitchen protocol to borrowed books, a house party requires certain considerations from all if it is to be one of ease and enjoyment—without ruffled feathers, gnashing teeth and "boudoir murmurs."

Socializing

As a Guest

It takes effort to be a houseguest. Come prepared to contribute to the comaraderie and esprit of the weekend and to carry your fair share of responsibility in seeing that the weekend works.

- Make it a point to get to know and take an interest in other guests; presumably they are there because they mean something to the host and hostess, even if they would not have been your own choice.

- Mix and mingle. You were invited for your company, not to lock yourself away in a bedroom for hours on end.

- Look for opportunities to create or enhance the congeniality of the weekend. Have a funny story to tell, a few new jokes.

- Don't monopolize the host and hostess, attempting to exclude other guests.

- Avoid sensitive subjects that might fuel dissension. If discussions do get heated, back out of a conversation. This is not your time or place to "take a stand" and persist in an uncomfortable situation.

- Go with the flow. If the host has planned a blitz-krieg of social happenings, athletic activities and cultural exchanges, go along happily. Or, if you have been left to your own devices, get creative.

- At a weekend party, houseguests should resist acting "clubby" when outsiders attend. Introduce yourself to yet another set of your host's friends, understanding that gracious behavior dictates your role as a second host.

- Invite or include other guests in independent activities. Adopt the attitude that "any friend of yours is a friend of mine."

As a Host

- If entertaining a group that doesn't know one another, proper planning and organizing become critical to permit you the time to mix and nurse people.

- Considerate manners dictate that a host not impose religious or political convictions on his "captive audience."

- In pre-weekend communications or at the start of the weekend, give each guest a little background on the other. This insight serves both to heighten the anticipation and act as an icebreaker when guests do meet.

- Good conversation is an integral part of a successful weekend; take the time and focus on introductions, providing interesting snippets and anecdotes that start exchanges on a high note.

> *NOTE: Designing a weekend guest list deserves particular attention because everyone is going to be together 16 hours a day for two to three days.*

Taking Leave

◆ Remember the old saw about guests and fish. Limit your stay to **three days.**

◆ Arrive *after* and leave *before* the hostess.

◆ Don't forget anything. Few things are more annoying to a host than looking for the right box, worrying over packing materials, standing in line at the post office.

◆ Communicate your thanks by phone or letter within two weeks.

◆ If the arrival/departure point is a long distance from the house (45-minutes drive, plus) plan to arrange your own transportation to and from.

◆ Don't miss your flight or train.

Other Invitations

This is one of the cardinal rules of weekend entertaining: Don't accept an invitation, no matter how tempting, that doesn't include your host/guest. In some situations it is appropriate to ask ahead about guest's/host's plans. Would they like to join you or do something on their own? But at no point does a host go off to another engagement without making arrangements for their guests—food in the fridge, reservations at a restaurant.

And guests do not come with their own social calendar in hand, using their host's home as a command post for their pre-planned social outings.

Children and Pets

It is a common courtesy that a guest does not appear with children or pets in tow unless they have been specifically invited. An entire weekend can be thrown off in pace, scheduling and tone by the unexpected addition of a child. And when either are included, it is the guest's responsibility to provide any special needs (i.e., formula or kitty litter).

Under no circumstances should a child or pet become a disruptive element in a weekend. Conversely, the host owes it to his guests to spare them from misbehaving pets. No dogs that jump up with muddy paws, chew shoes, run off with chiffon dresses— and no ill-mannered children—who sing or dance or otherwise attempt to entertain; spy on or eavesdrop; throw tantrums or distract the host from guest; play dirty tricks.

Appropriate Dress

As a Host

A hostess's written or verbal discussions with her guests should always include this subject . . . particularly if they are coming from a different culture or part of the country. You otherwise take the chance of discomfort, both physical and emotional, on a guest's part.

The easiest way to handle this is to describe, generally, what you will be wearing. Stay away from interpretive statements like "casual," with no further details. "Casual" in one place can mean jeans and a T-shirt; in another it might call for a silk blouse and Bulgari jewelry.

✦ Be sure to mention any activities that would require special clothing *(We like to hike and have found that running shoes get too slippery on the mossy trails.")*.

✦ Don't forget any social taboos (the club does not permit ladies to wear shorts or slacks; all-whites must be worn on the tennis courts).

✦ Gauge your guest and make specific suggestions, in their best interest, so they won't feel over- or under-dressed *("I loved that blue dress you wore at the Luptons. Why don't you bring that for dinner Saturday night"*—for the guest who never gets out of jeans. *"We're very casual. You probably won't even need any jewelry"*—for the friend who overdoses on glitz).

As a Guest

"Appropriate Dress" means selections that dovetail as closely with the hostess's comments as possible, especially if she has made a point of being very specific. It is a compliment to your host to attempt to be sympatico in dress and, conversely, a slight, if you are not sensitive to the occasion or circumstances.

◇ At least convey the impression that you have given careful thought to what you are wearing. Give the appearance of being "pulled together": be sure your clothes are clean, shoes in good repair, hems and seams mended, and that they coordinate well.

◇ Bring enough so you don't have to keep borrowing.

◇ Don't plan to appear at any time in your pajamas and bathrobe unless your friendship and the guest list merit it.

◇ If you'll be sharing a bath with others and walking to and from, bring a better bathrobe than you normally bump around in at home.

Telephone Manners

Come prepared to manage your long distance phone needs without any inconvenience to the host. Both touch tone phones and the wide selection of long distance companies have simplified the issue of making long distance calls from someone else's phone. There is no excuse today for a guest to commit that annoying faux pas of running up a phone bill, only to make some off-hand remark about "let me know what my charges are when your bill comes in."

☎ If you are going out of the country, get an international calling card number.

☎ Don't turn a host's house, and phone, into your business office.

☎ Don't turn a host's house, and phone, into your social center.

☎ Avoid, or limit the calls coming in for you. Few hosts, or their staff, enjoy the role of message taker for a guest.

Ailing Guests

It's embarrassing enough that they are encumbered in their efforts to be charming. As the host, be empathic and sensitive to their plight—don't take it personally as a slight or show of ingratitude.

On the other hand, as a guest, don't come if you are sick. If you are stricken during the weekend, be sensitive to infecting others and excuse yourself to your room.

Neatness

Despite what your own home and bath might suffer in this area, there is only one way that a host's living space should be kept—neat and tidy.

◇ Consign your clothes, running shoes, duffels to your bedroom only.

◇ Keep track of your personal possessions to avoid the annoying habit of leaving something behind.

◇ If you read the newspaper, or start a project, don't leave it strewn about.

◇ When sharing a bath, keep your sundry toiletries together in one kit, putting them back as you use them.

◇ Don't spread out all over the sink and bath.

◇ Wipe the sink after you are finished.

◇ If you remove or borrow something, put it back where you found it.

◇ Make your bed each day. When you leave, determine from your host whether you should make the bed, strip the bed, change linens and make the bed or leave as is.

◇ Do not decide to re-decorate, or re-organize any part of the host's home without a specific go-ahead.

◇ Upon departing, leave your room exactly as it was when you arrived.

Around the House

In the Kitchen:

➨ Assist, yes, but don't take over. Respect the host's plans, menus and recipes.

➨ Unless you have been given carte blanche to invade the refrigerator and freezer, tread carefully. You may be eating the makings of tomorrow's lunch.

➨ If you have special dietary needs, bring them.

➨ Some servants can be territorial about "their" kitchen and don't care to have guests intruding. In other situations, protocol would dictate that guests never go near the kitchen area.

In the Bath:

The guest's bath may also be the same one that any visitors or party attendees would be using. Therefore, keep it clean and picked up at all times—especially on the night of a party.

With a houseful of guests, keep your shower time to a considerate minimum.

In the Laundry:

✑ Unless you're a family member, don't even *consider* bringing your week's worth of laundry for the host or staff to have to deal with.

✑ Determine first if you can use the washer and dryer for weekend dirty clothes.

✑ If there is staff to see to your clothes, ask upon arrival how much notice they need to launder clothes, press a dress for Saturday night's party, repair a tear.

Miscellaneous

■ **Return borrowed books**
(at over $19.95 for a hardcover book,
we're not talking peanuts). At the least,
offer to exchange value for value—
"I'll trade _____ for _____."

■ **Sharing responsibilities as a hosting couple—**
The burden should not fall too heavily on one shoulder,
particularly when it comes to guiding or escorting guests.
For this permits the stay-at-home team member some
welcome personal, quiet time.

Drop-by Guests
Always call first. No one enjoys being caught unaware, especially when their attention is already devoted to houseguests.
With the courtesy of a little notice, a friend can accord the caller
an unhurried and gracious welcome.

Tipping

Want to be invited back? Read the following carefully:

It is customary for a houseguest, whether spending one night,
one weekend or one week, to "remember" the servants—and
required if you are spending one week or more.

While the amount is dependent upon the level and quantity of
service (were you cooked three meals a day or just dinner? Were
your beds changed daily and clothes pressed?), the ACT of
tipping is an expected gesture. And not only is it courteous, it is
also a compliment to your host. Give it careful thought. Servants
can tip the balance of power in your favor, or undermine your
efforts to return.

Servants today are too difficult to come by for any hostess to
excuse less than the best intentions and manners toward them on
the part of a guest—particularly if, as in many cases, they are
considered family members.

Some tips on tipping:

✪ Is your destination a very grand abode, with many servants? Tactfully include the dollar value of tips in a pre-visit discussion with your host. This eliminates the chance of shock on your part (at $250 for a week's stay you might consider canceling) and ensures that you will have enough cash.

✪ Different locales and cultures necessitate an individualized approach, so even if you are an experienced traveler and houseguest, ask your host. If not comfortable asking the host, seek out another guest who has stayed before.

✪ Tip in the currency of the country.

✪ Put the gratuity in an *envelope*, with a *note*, if only a one-liner. Then further personalize the gesture by giving it directly to the individual. (When a number of servants are concerned, an alternative would be to give one amount to the host or house major domo for distribution on a percentage basis that they would determine).

CAUTION.: Overtipping can be as much of a faux pas as not tipping at all. Here again, it's sage advice to get some direction from the host ("I was planning on giving Rosa $10 and Kile $25. Do you feel that's appropriate?"). Otherwise, you may run the risk of throwing off a delicate economic balance that the host has developed. (Your $25 tip may make the host's established salary look paltry).

In short, if your sizable gratuity causes a palace coup among the servants, you can forget any future invitations.

The Guest Who Would Not Go

OR *How to gracefully and assertively say goodbye*

Part and parcel of any guest's obligation is to be specific about the tenure of their stay, adjusting the date to meet with the approval of a host. But certainly, a guest's inherent obligation is to cease to be a guest at some point. If that comes later than sooner, and your verbal or written time frame has been ignored, here are some suggestions for speeding that fixture on its way.

- *_____ is arriving in two days and I must air and ready the guest room(s).*

- *My mother-in-law is arriving in two days and it has always been understood that she would have the entire house to herself, along with our undivided attention.*

- *The house is being bombed for fleas, and we all must get out or three days.*

- *My annual big housecleaning is about to take place and the crews will only work in a vacated house.*

- *The water is going to be shut off for a few days for a plumbing repair.*

POSTSCRIPT:
The Seven Deadly Sins of an Ill-Mannered Houseguest

1. Arrive early, stay late, miss the train, ferry, plane.

2. Bring dog, cat, children, Aunt Molly.

3. Never offer to help.

4. Go off to social events without including the host.

5. Sit around, waiting to be entertained and whining, "What is there to do?"

6. Freeload—poach liquor, clothes, books, spouse.

7. Try to pirate household help.

Opining on Au Pairs

Au pairs, nannies, mother's helpers. While they are known by different names, their responsibilities differ only by degrees. And as they become more a part of busy households today, they likewise become an issue in weekend entertaining.

Two points of protocol that help smooth the way:

1. Guests should not plan on including an au pair in the weekend plans unless it has been discussed and cleared with the hostess.
  - ↫ Some hosts feel that this is tantamount to an uninvited guest and an inconvenience. (Au pairs seldom clean up or fix meals, but do require another bed).

2. Respect the rules of the host's household.
  - ↫ For example, whether the au pair eats with children, or adults; what the au pair can join in or not be included in; where she sleeps.
  - ↫ A host should be comfortable setting parameters, from which point a guest may decide not to include the au pair.

Further points for good communications:

- ↦ To head off problems, any initial hiring discussion should include the need for some flexibility on the au pair's part regarding weekend entertaining (i.e., when guests come, au pair will move into child's room) and that additional responsibilities may occasionally be included in selected situations (i.e., weekend visits).

- ↦ Any selected "additional responsibilities" should be accompanied by time off or money.

- ↦ It is an unwritten rule that a hostess/guest does not give direction to another's au pair.

- ↦ An au pair is responsible only for taking care of her charges, not someone else's children.

- Thus a host or guest should plan on providing a sitter for their children (i.e., when adults go out for dinner) unless specific arrangements have been agreed to between au pair and sponsor.

- Meals and sleeping accommodations for the guest's au pair should be factored in by the host.

- Miscellaneous expenses (admissions, snacks, etc.) should be given to an au pair up front.

- Do not tip another's au pair unless you have first cleared it with her sponsor.

SHORT SUBJECT

Is This Any Way to Treat a Weekend?

Weekends are meant to refresh, but too many of us project our weekday freneticism onto those two precious days. Whether we feel guilty about simply relaxing or fear that we'll have lost our edge come Monday morning, too many of us are activity addicts.

Try leaving one day totally unplanned and "go with the flow." Doctors suggest this self-pampering is not only good for the psyche but makes for renewed energy when the weekday comes.

Good Form

Invitation Pointers

This is your first opportunity to set the tone of the weekend—
and forestall the clash of expectations that can make for uncomfortable times.

♦ *Be specific.* Don't assume anything, especially if this is a
guest's first visit in your weekend abode. After all, it's only
human nature to want to know what you have to look
forward to.

♦ *How to avoid any possibility of an overstaying guest?*
Make mention (as tactfully, or as pointedly, as the situation
calls for) of "leave taking" in your invitation. If necessary,
include or forward train or ferry schedules with departures
underlined. And the guest who has been extended a some-
what open-ended invitation should let the hostess know
ahead of time when she is planning to arrive, *and* depart: "I'll
be there by 9:00 p.m. Friday and leave 2:00 p.m. Sunday."

To include in your invitation:
✔ Phone number where guest can be reached during the
weekend.
✔ Clear notes on clothing needs and style of dress.
✔ Planned activities, side trips, options.
✔ Necessary sports gear.
✔ Notes and background on other guests.
✔ Suggestions on travel logistics, referrals, approximate
costs.
✔ Written directions and/or map.
✔ Climate observations.

Additional enclosures:
✓ Special notes (i.e., no restaurants accept credit cards;
customs is a bit of a joke but is taken very seriously by
customs officers, so do be earnest).
✓ Fax and telex numbers.
✓ History or background on region.
✓ Local practices to be aware of (i.e., there is a terrible speed
trap right after you turn onto Highway 213).

Some notes on writing thank-you notes

•◦ You don't have to write an epistle. Any note—if only three creative sentences—is better than no "thank-you" at all.

•◦ Try to avoid starting the note with "I."

•◦ Don't be concerned that a note is too informal. People are always pleased with any expressions that seem friendly and spontaneous.

•◦ Avoid generic prose. Use details, cite specific incidents, refer to something by name.

•◦ Got a case of writer's block? Loosen up by pretending that you are writing a best friend thanking her for the good time that you have had. Then substitute the hostess's name in the salutation and close with an appropriate ending.

Invitation Samples

Hostess to Guest Invitation, simple, yet covers issues of arrival and departure.

Griffin,

Looking forward to seeing you around 4'ish on Saturday. Some friends from Covington (Bill W. wrote the definitive book on the history of our little town) have been invited for dinner at 7:00. Although we don't dress formally down here, Jonathan is of the school that believes a coat and tie should be worn to the table. Sundays are for sleeping in and then enjoying a late bountiful Southern breakfast. After that, of course, we will all take a country walk before saying our good-byes.

À bientôt,

Hostess to Guest Invitation, with a potpourri of details:

Dear Jonathan and Bettie:

Smokey and I are absolutely delighted that you will be joining us in Mustique! We have taken a beautiful house in a lovely setting on top of a hill with a spectacular view of the Caribbean, and, from what I hear, it comes with an excellent staff to look after your every wish and whim! The house has two swimming pools, and a (possibly completed) tennis court.

Mustique is a privately-owned island and not easily reachable by regular air service. The best connection is for you to get to Barbados (or to St. Vincent) and continue by private charter to Mustique. The charters are managed by Mustique Air and are perfectly safe and comfortable. I have called Mustique this past week and have obtained the following information on private charters:

* * *

Smokey and I will pick you up at the "airport" when you arrive and drive you over to the house. You will have to clear customs in Mustique—it's a bit of a joke, but is taken very seriously by the customs officer, so please try to be quite earnest about it. We will expect you on February 19th and let you go (regretfully) on February 26th.

Since the house is fully staffed, you won't have to do a thing except let your imagination guide you. If you are interested in snorkeling, please bring your own gear. If you want to do some scuba diving, equipment and boat charters can be arranged on the island. If you like to play tennis, the Cotton House Club has tennis courts available, if ours isn't finished yet. There is also fishing and horseback riding available. If you still feel very energetic, arrangements can be made to visit nearby islands by boat or by private plane—it is all easily available and is only a matter of cost and your special interests.

Please remember that Mustique is a small island and everything has to be brought over from St. Vincent or elsewhere. Vodka, gin and rum are easily available and quite cheap. If you prefer bourbon or whiskey please bring a bottle—or two or three— with you since it will be both difficult and very expensive to buy locally.

As far as dress code is concerned, it will be very casual during the day. The weather will be quite hot and the sun is treacherous at midday, so please bring a hat and lots of sunscreen lotion. In the evening the ladies will be asked to look ravishing in beautiful long caftans or pants and tops, and flowers in their hair. Since no one will be looking at the men anyway, they will be able to get away with white slacks and silk shirt (no coats or ties ever!).

In case you are so sorely missed that you need to be called in Mustique, here is the address and phone number _____.

All my love,

Bread and Butter Letters

Hostess to Guest

Thank-you for house gift

✉

Jules,

You are the master of the weekend house gift! And I certainly don't have to ask "How did you know we needed it?" Were you aware, though, that a toaster-oven is particularly handy when toasting pita pockets . . .?

We loved having you back and especially enjoyed meeting Lorraine. I hope the weekend proved eventful, even though you didn't win the tournament.

Merci beaucoup for your clever and thoughtful gift. I'm sure many of our other houseguests will thank you, too. Keep us posted on your "new" business.

Hostess to Guest

Thank-you, for food and cooking duties

✉

John,

Here's hoping that your species is not endangered. Honestly, appearing laden with exotic foods, then thrilling everyone with your culinary skills, then cleaning up after yourself . . . who do I think I am, a guest at my own house party?? Bless you! And a million thank you's—from all who were lucky enough to share this weekend with the quintessential houseguest.

Hugs,

Dear Charlotte,

A gardening and thank-you gift is FINALLY on its way to you—I'm embarrassed that you did not receive it May 20 as planned, but the store made a series of errors that scotched my good intentions.

At any rate, do hope you can use it . . . to and from the weekend house as well as at home. We think of you often and extol the virtues of Montreal and its stellar residents to all we meet.

See you soon?

Love,

Guest to Hostess

Thank-you for weekend, with accompanying gift

April,

Champagne will do it for me every time! Thanks for the bubbly greeting and the de-lish dinner. Above and beyond the call of duty, and the frosting on top of an already superlative evening given the company. I'm surprised, but thrilled that it worked out for the three of us on the same evening . . . the highlight of my weekend.

Plus, your apartment looks grand! Thanks again for the treats—I enjoyed every sip and bite along with the much-appreciated room and board.

Guest to Hostess

Thank-you for busy weekend when schedule permitted only one evening together

Guest to Hostess

Thank-you for
weekend in
the city

✉

Dear Grandmama,

Yet another achievement to add to that long list—and growing daily (the list, too). Thanks so very much for making a houseguest out of me, complete with my own bed and bath. I fully appreciate what that means in New York City. Loved the luxury and particulary the chance to spend quality time catching up—

I'll keep you posted on "the project"!

Guest to Hostess

Thank-you
for being
included in
a last minute
holiday
get-together

✉

Caroline,

Back in Boston now, but I wanted you to know how much I enjoyed being with you again after all these years. A bit of serendipity that seemed to characterize this Easter— and make it so special.

Thank you so for making me indeed feel like a family member. Bedding down with Suzanne gave me the welcome opportunity to see the world through the eyes of a 12-year-old. I was enchanted with her wit and perception!

Good luck in your new and well-timed career—let's compare notes soon.

Dear Bettie,

Every moment at "The Waves" was a perfect delight! So much so that my work at the office this morning qualifies as a zero in efficiency; perhaps it is just as well, if I am to remain employed, that the average weekend in the country is different—very.

Thank you so much for including me. As fate would have it, I ran into Patsy and Charlie at lunch Tuesday. We immediately had a three-some conversation on the wonderful time we all had over the weekend.

Cordially,

Guest to Hostess

(from a guest who did not know the hostess, but was the guest of another guest)

Margie,

Every time I return from The Waves, I am reminded again that there is no house to which I always go with so much pleasure and leave on Sunday with so much regret.

Warmest appreciation and affection!

Guest to Hostess

A quick note.

GREAT WEEKEND ENTERTAINING

IV

WEEKEND "TO DO'S"

WEEKEND TO DO'S

The Activities Book

The first blush of greetings has faded, the guests have settled in and that unspoken question hangs in the air—"What's there to do?"

The savvy host will, of course, first offer up his personalized, well-researched and quite conclusive scrapbook of to do's and activities (that is, if you're perfect—but if you're mortal, like the rest of us, it will be in varying states of preparedness and update. Which is still better than no notes at all . . .). Well worth the investment in time, "The Activities Book" will give guests the impression that you have considered their every need. It would include, but should not be limited, to:

- a map of the area with points of interest highlighted (have plenty of Xeroxed copies on hand)

- a listing of local museums, historic houses, institutions with their hours and, preferably, informative pamphlets with color photos

- a selection of "day-trippin'" options in the surrounding countryside and towns

- spots for great views— and great photographs

- notes and hours of shopping opportunities, to include special categories like antiques and discount stores

- comments and ratings on local restaurants, plus notes on dress suggestions and credit card payment

- landmarks, both literally and "local interest" (i.e., the old-fashioned, town "movie palace," a throwback to everyone's childhood)

- a listing of gardens, nurseries, garden centers and observations on local flora and fauna

- local tour brochures and your personal suggestions of two, three or four-hour tour combinations

- specific children's activities list

Additional Helpful Hints:

❧ Save the arts and enter-tainment section of the local Sunday paper for next weekend's Friday arrivals.

❧ Subscribe to the "Gallery Guide" for art aficionados.

❧ If in the country, have a horticulture friend write out a walking tour of local flora and fauna.

❧ Make specific note of activities and options that are indigenous to the locale and circumstances, and different from what guests would typically be doing back home (i.e., visiting the fish market auctions at 4:00 a.m., hitting the 6:00 a.m. flea market).

❧ Arrange for a behind-the-scenes private viewing of a local product in manu-facture (candy cane fac-tory, salmon smoking and packaging, marzipan kitchen).

❧ Schedule a cooking class with a local chef making native dishes with regional ingredients.

❧ Or line up lessons in activities that will be tak-ing place over the week-end—skeet shooting, croquet, bocci ball.

❧ Include guests in garden-ing pursuits: tending topi-aries, harvesting pecans, planting an allée of trees (each one named for a guest).

S HORT SUBJECT

Road Trippin'

So jump in that convertible, pop on a Donegal tweed cap, strap on the picnic hamper and head out for a tour of local color. And don't forget to include strategic stops along the way—a local pub for Irish coffee, a hilltop to watch the sunset. Every guest wants a feeling for the surrounding countryside, the local habitats, highlights of architecture. It helps one to feel "oriented." And if you've got a fabulous fun car—new convertible, old Morgan, classic Mercedes, Woody station wagon—all the better.

> *NOTE:* "The Activities Book" also serves as a welcome memory jogger for the weekend host who draws a blank while trying to orchestrate what passes for a Chinese fire drill.

Flower Ladies Weekend

Friday:
Alan Haskell Nursery (picnic lunch)
Peckham's Nursery
Dinner @ Folksail, Little Campion

Saturday:
"Secret Garden" Tour and Tea
Lunch at the Plumb Line
Dinner at the Waves

Sunday:
Green Animals Topiary Gardens (picnic lunch)
4:00 p.m. Tea with Newport Flower Ladies
Dinner at Newport Grill

J U N E ❧ 1 9 9 1

In special situations, with dear friends around whose personal interests the weekend has been planned, it's fun to greet them with a "dance card"—all the better if it's hand-lettered.

Games People Play

Don't overlook the welcome assist that assorted sports and games can give you in your weekend entertaining efforts. Make it a point to develop an inventory and add to it regularly. Guests will welcome them—who doesn't love "toys"?—and *you* will welcome a self-reliant guest.

Many need no more than nature's own—a small plot of lawn, tall oak or elm, level dirt. And none require a bank loan or arsenal of equipment.

A selection of games and sports that guests can fall into on their own and without assistance:

▲ right and left-handed boomerang

▲ croquet

▲ badminton

▲ ping pong

▲ bumper pool

▲ volleyball

▲ horseshoes

▲ shuffleboard

▲ bocci ball—traditional Italian lawn game

▲ English lawn bowling

▲ trampoline

▲ checkers and backgammon on large-scaled boards or painted floorcloth

▲ tree swing

▲ archery

▲ darts

▲ baseball

▲ and a hammock . . . for the serious sport of sleeping

PARDEE TIP

Keep a jigsaw puzzle going in a convenient location for guests to play at for five minutes—or five hours.

Social Games and Other Diversions

They're back! Both board games and "parlor" games have rekindled new opportunities for socializing. For in our hectic, daily lives, the kind of activities that people enjoy most are those that involve interaction with others; and the most popular are the light, noncompetitive games where it matters little whether you win or lose, but whether you had FUN.

So enjoy these favorites from the '50s, when social intercourse and the art of conversation were as polished as Fred and Ginger.

Pencil and Paper Games

✤ **PERSONAL ANALOGIES** ✤

The object: Paying compliments
and paying off old scores:

✎ Write the names of those present vertically down a sheet of paper.

✎ Each guest, in turn, then chooses a subject—i.e., color, food, drink, street, material—which all guests write horizontally across the top of their paper.

✎ Then everyone writes alongside each person's name the nearest analogy he can think of for each different subject.

✎ Each takes turns reading his sheet out loud, explaining his selection *if he* wishes.

> Example: For Bettie,
> color = red
> food = peach melba
> drink = Lillet
> street = Commonwealth
> material = shantung silk

❧ CATEGORIES ❧

Easy, perhaps, but no one ever makes
a grade of 100 on this one. Set a time limit.
The object: To fill up all four words for each
of the designated categories.

☞ A four-letter word is chosen by the person whose turn it is.

☞ Each player writes it in capitals vertically down the left margin of the paper.

☞ Then each player provides a category (presumably one in which he will excel), such as American musicians, Roman emperors, perennial flowers, beverages.

☞ Players quickly write down a selection for each category beginning with the four initial letters provided.

EXAMPLE:

The word chosen is **GNAT**; the category is "beverages."
Selections: grappa, nescafe, Asti, Tanqueray.

❧ TELEGRAMS ❧

Among a group of friends, this private telegram
can be an amusing tongue-in-cheek adventure—
perhaps insinuating something of the circumstances
that await an expected guest. Set a time limit.
The object: To write the 12-letter telegram
in the given time frame.

✐ Write a given 12-letter word, in capitals, vertically down the paper.

✐ A theme is set, a recipient (known to everyone) is selected and each player has to write a telegram.

✐ The words of the telegram have to begin with and be in the same sequence as the given 12-letter word; the first two and last two letters may be used to designate recipient and sender.

EXAMPLE:

CHIMNEYPIECE; theme is "state of affairs in Washington."
Telegram: "Cheney has influenza Meese needed
examination yesterday President informed
England (signed) Conference Executive.

Parlor Games

❈ **DOG AND BONE** ❈

A game for two . . . a handkerchief for one . . .
5 points to win.
The object : To get back to *either* wall ("home")
with the handkerchief without being touched by the
opponent (2 points); *or* by a pretended pick-up,
to induce your opponent to touch you when you
have not got the handkerchief (1 point);
or to touch the opponent while he is carrying
the handkerchief home (1 point).

☞ Both players stand with backs against the wall, facing each other; a handkerchief is placed on the floor, midway between opponents.

☞ At the word "Go," both approach the handkerchief.

☞ Note that if a player has once touched the handkerchief, he cannot drop it but must try to get "home" (which, on either wall, shouldn't be more than 4 feet wide and should be clearly defined by unbreakable objects.)

❈ **ADVERBS** ❈

A fun pantomime game requiring no props
or previous preparation.
The object: For one player to guess
the key adverb or adverbial phrase
by analyzing the actions of the others.

★ The player of the moment leaves the room while the rest decide on one word or phrase that describes a way of acting (i.e., "miserably," "like a fox," "mysteriously").

★ When the player returns, he asks each individual to act in a manner that will key him to the adverb.

★ The acting continues 'til he guesses the adverb from his fellow players' pantomime.

| ❃ | **HURDLES** | ❃ |

This is a talking game, great as an icebreaker
at a party or a good assist for meal-times
if the guest list is challenging.
The object: To identify the mystery character.

➤ The player of the moment thinks of a person, place or thing, announcing the letter with which it starts.

➤ The others have to guess what it is by asking questions, or crossing the hurdle.

➤ The challenging part of this game is that the player of the moment must qualify his "no" with a word that starts with the letter of his subject. Should he be stumped, the others can then ask a "business" question, i.e., a question concerning the nature of the player's subject.

EXAMPLE:
Subject: "Madonna"
Q: Are you a composer? A: No, I'm not Mozart.
Q: Are you a city? A: No, I'm not Minneapolis.
Business question: Do you live on the West Coast?

| ❃ | **I SEE** | ❃ |

A child's game that is delightful
for grown-ups, too . . . and particularly handy as
an icebreaker at the beginning of a party;
also a good excuse for pairing people up.
The object: For guests to locate all 20 hidden items in a
stipulated period of time. A talent for camouflage
makes the game that much more conversational.

✪ Hide 20 small objects in a room that will be out of bounds 'til the search begins (a stamp pasted on the label of a bottle, a rubber band around a door knob, a gold ring on a lamp finial).

✪ The rule is that players must be able to see each thing on the list without moving or touching anything.

✪ Distribute lists to player, with pencils, and start the clock!

Great for punsters . . . and a hostess to whom
matchmaking is a fine science.
The object: To identify both members
of a conversational team whose actual meeting
might be described as highly unlikely.

✖ Two players, chosen to be the "improbable pair," leave the
room to decide on their identities.

✖ When they return, they hold a conversation in front of the
others, always talking in character within which are woven
clues to their names.

EXAMPLE: Jimmy Hoffa to Joan of Arc: *"How do you feel about steak
(stake)?"* Joan: *"I don't like it hot, but you'd better move on, I think
I see a cop."*

✖ The audience should ask leading questions designed to
confirm their suspicion about the two characters without
tipping off anyone else. (To Joan: "Weren't you awfully
burned up at one point?")

✖ Questions continue until both characters are identified; the
two audience members who have guessed correctly become
the next "improbable pair."

| ❀ **CLUMPS AND THUMPS** ❀ |

A lively game, with its own cadence.
The object: For one side to totally absorb
the other team.

♦ Two seven-man teams (or "clumps") stand facing each other;
the team captains have a stick.

♦ Choose a broad topic (i.e., "creatures" = animal, bird, fish
or insect).

♦ A member of one team calls the name of any "creatures"
subject beginning with the letter "A." His captain immediately begins to count (slowly) to 10, thumping the floor with
his stick at each count.

♦ Before the captain reaches 10, an opposing team member
must retaliate with another creature beginning with "A";
then the second captain begins to count and thump, while the
first side thinks of a new beast.

♦ When one team wins, because the other has run out of "A's,"
it may choose a member of the losing team and add him/her
to its number.

♦ Then the teams continue through the alphabet 'til one side
has been absorbed by the other.

NOTE: Captains are allowed to call like the rest; but if two
members of a side call out different names together, the
opposing side may instantly claim the second name given.

```
┌─────────────────────────────────────────────┐
│        ❦    THREE STEPS    ❦                  │
└─────────────────────────────────────────────┘
```

A scintillating parlor game . . . even better
when taken out of doors to the wide open spaces.
The object: To eliminate all players until only
one remains, the victor skilled at using only
three steps to avoid entrapment.

◊   Players scatter themselves, each placing himself at a distance
of a least three large paces from his nearest neighbor.

◊   The Master of Ceremonies, with the name of each player on
separate slips, goes around passing a slip to each player.

◊   The name on the slip is that player's prey, to be caught with
slow, calculated cunning.

◊   But that player (i.e., "A") is, at the same time, someone else's
prey.

◊   The MC then reads out the names of each player and *each in
turn* takes three steps (a step can only be a walking step—
no leaps or reversing steps).

◊   "A" must catch his prey by touching him without falling
over; "B" is then out of the game and gives his slip to "A,"
with the name of the player that "A" is now going after.

Electronic Entertainment

It's here to stay . . . and it makes staying home an adventure in itself. For weekend retreats, where entertaining literally means creating "amusements" for guests, video and audiocassettes offer you a wealth of options.

From your local video store, from mail order catalogs (like "Wireless"), from specialty interest stores (like Sharper Image), now's the time to start your electronic library. Just a small sampling of what's available:

Videocassettes

The Great Gleason
A 90-minute extravaganza for fans of the Golden Age of Jackie Gleason. Hundreds of unreleased original film clips, including never-before-seen "Honeymooners" footage. Also includes classic live bloopers and gags, plus ad-libbed slapstick with Art Carney.

The March of Time American Lifestyles
Newsreels produced by *Time* magazine from 1935-1951 giving moviegoers a look at what was happening in America and around the world. Rare original black and white newsreel footage shows how Americans lived, learned, played, aged, ate, shopped, dressed and more, set against the turbulent backdrop of the war and postwar eras.

Reader's Digest Great National Parks
You can experience the beauty and majesty of America's greatest national parks—Grand Canyon, Yosemite and Yellowstone. Each video is a personal tour complete with sights, sounds and spectacular moments: from running rapids to hang gliding high above rocky cliffs, watching sunsets and witnessing the changing seasons.

Train Videos
A must-have for every train buff's library. The history and restoration of great locomotives, combined with breathtaking photography featuring engineers putting each train through its paces.

Top Guns: The Real Pilots. The Real Story

Find out what it's like to go through spin training, water survival, carrier night landings and the Top Gun Fighter School. Stunning air footage cut to exciting rock music: the real story of life as a top gun.

Around-the-World Travel Videos

The kind of trips you'd like to take yourself—with *no* annoying commercials. Fascinating, enlightening and full of memorable images and facts, each runs 43-60 minutes. Travel to England's Yorkshire Dales, Paris, Egypt, or go on safari in Kenya, ride the Orient Express.

Play Bridge with Omar Sharif

A bridge player's dream come true: you can play 15 challenging hands with a world-class bridge champion as your partner. For each hand, you make the bids, you decide on a plan of action and then Sharif takes you step by step through the game.

Isaac Asimov's Robots Mystery Game

Solve a murder mystery in deep space. Who did it? An Earthling? A Spacer? Or a robot? Based on Asimov's Robot novels, "Robots" provides hours of fun for 1 to 12 players, ages 10 and up. And you never play the same game twice.

Audubon Society's Birds of America Videos

The only video series that combines birds in flight, bird calls and sounds, computer-animated range maps and stills by master nature photographers. These meticulously researched guides will help you positively identify 505 different species.

Audiocassettes

"You Sing the Hits"

Put yourself and your guests in the spotlight with these clever cassettes. Side A features a vocalist, with instrumental back-up and six popular songs by famous composers; side B contains stereo background tracks only (no vocals). Practice with side A until you've mastered the songs, then flip to side B and you're an instant singing star.

"The Shadow" Cassettes

Who knows what evil lurks in the hearts of men? Anyone who listened to radio knows "The Shadow" was one of the most popular shows to ever chill the airwaves. Each of the eight episodes is an original radio broadcast starring Orson Welles—the first Shadow.

"Radio's Greatest Comedies" Cassettes

Enjoy a nostalgic trip to the 1930s, '40s, and early '50s when comedy was king and radio was in its Golden Age. These are original, unedited, radio shows, including commercials, featuring such treats as Jack Benny, Fibber McGee and Molly, Burns and Allen, Amos and Andy, Groucho Marx's "You Bet Your Life" and W. C. Fields' skits.

"The New Adventures of Sherlock Holmes"

Original radio broadcasts from the mid-1940s, lost for over 40 years until recently discovered and re-released. Complete with commercials, haunting organ music, sound effects and a full cast of characters led by Basil Rathbone and Nigel Bruce. Be amazed again by Sherlock Holmes through such episodes as "The Unfortunate Tobacconist," "The Viennese Strangler," "The Notorious Canary Trainer," "The Strange Adventure of the Uneasy Easy Chair," and more.

Rainy Day Tips

Into every host's life a drop of rain must fall . . . Don't push the panic button when your planned activities run afoul of gray skies. To keep you from feeling under siege, keep these options handy:

❖ Pull out the *Mensa Genius Quiz Book* and determine everyone's IQ.

❖ Grab a cookbook for a team effort assault on the kitchen.

❖ Play spin-the-bottle, pin-the-tail-on-the-donkey.

❖ Turn on Michael Jackson and play musical chairs.

❖ Shoot trap off the back porch.

❖ Distribute copies of Shakespeare for guests to pick out seven one-liners to characterize themselves as they would like to be known.

❖ Go on an indoor scavenger hunt.

❖ Round up old clothes and odds and ends for a create-your-own-costume party.

❖ Have a "literary lions" book report hour.

❖ Play "60 Minutes," where each guest discusses and/or demonstrates a favorite subject.

❖ Make one spectacular dessert (i.e., a gingerbread house or Martha Washington's Great Cake).

❖ Ask each guest to bring a favorite poem for a poetry reading hour.

❖ Invite a local historian in to discourse on the architecture of the environs, political history, special points of interest.

Or that rainy day may inspire some philosophical soul searching. If so, create an environment that encourages people to divulge their secret side and suppressed desires. This will give guests an opportunity to learn about each other, while at the same time nurturing empathy and sympathy.

Try what we have nicknamed "Dreamscapes":

"EARLY REFORMATIONS"—*If you were 21 again, what would you do differently?*

"CASTAWAYS"—*If you were shipwrecked on a desert island, what record, book, food and frivolity would you want?*

"HEART THROBS"—*What is your choice, and why, for the sexiest person for each of the last five centuries?*

"HEROES AND HEROINES"—*When it comes to survival, who rates and why?*

Some Things to Have on Hand for Rainy Days

▲ *Mensa Genius Quiz Book*
▲ *The New York Times World Atlas*
▲ Sonnets from Elizabeth Barrett Browning
▲ Poetry of Longfellow and Whitman
▲ Complete works of Shakespeare
▲ Garden catalogs
▲ Stress cassettes (actual sounds of nature to help relax and meditate, relieve insomnia, create a romantic mood)
▲ *Reader's Digest Guide to More than 1,000 Scenic and Interesting Places, Still Uncrowded and Inviting*
▲ *The Atlas of Mysterious Places*
▲ *The Dictionary of Misinformation*
▲ *Big Secrets: The Uncensored Truth About All Sorts of Stuff You Are Never Supposed to Know*
▲ Favorite board games—Monopoly, Scrabble, Risk, Trivial Pursuit, chess, checkers, etc.
▲ Decks of cards
▲ Ouija board

GREAT WEEKEND ENTERTAINING

V

A Sampling of
GREAT WEEKEND PARTIES

A SAMPLING OF
GREAT WEEKEND
THEME PARTIES

☞ PARTY CONCEPT
A Star-Studded Affair

The majority of us live in areas where the lights of the city and civilization hinder our ability to see the heavens. Short of actually going to a planetarium, who really has the opportunity to understand astronomy, to enjoy the facts behind the evening star, The Little Dipper, The Milky Way? This weekend is designed for participation from all invited. Assign each guest a small topic and let them do their homework. Then bring in some real experts to round out the program—an astrophysicist from a local university, the author of a book on related subjects, an armchair cosmologist with a flair for theatrics.

"Astronomy Awareness" could be another theme for the following day's Sunday brunch, to include the popular subject of astrology—the topic of compatability between star signs will always add a lively note to any house party. Other astronomy or astrology topics to consider:

- ✭ Folklore and fact revolving around Halley's Comet
- ✭ Was there *really* a star of Bethlehem?
- ✭ The constellations and Greek mythology
- ✭ Planetary activity that coincides with the end of a century

This party works any time of the year, but particularly from late spring to mid-fall when the weather permits dining under the stars.

THEME: *A Star-Studded Affair*

ATTIRE: Extra-terrestrial and/or diaphanous

INVITATION DESCRIPTION:
★ Eight-inch crescent moon, cut from deep blue card stock, with three-inch silver star suspended from the lower point of the moon. Inscription on the cutout moon—*"Come cast your moonglow over our weekend and we'll bring out the stars for you"*; party details written on star; small silver stars sprinkled in envelope.

DECORATIONS AND PROPS:
★ Candlearias (paper bags filled with sand and a candle) with star and crescent cutouts, lining the route to the party and/or tables
★ White, circular paper lanterns stencilled with moon and star motifs hanging from the trees
★ Photography prop of large ten-foot crescent moon, with seat cut into the plywood for a "languid portrait"

TABLE FORMAT AND SEATING:
★ Rectangular picnic tables, covered with a marine blue cotton duck cloth stencilled with big stars and crescent moons
★ Picnic benches with twelve-inch star cutouts thumbtacked to edge of bench creating illusion of chair back

---

P A R D E E   T I P

When dining outdoors . . .
A lawn or wide open space often lacks a sense of intimacy and coziness. Positioning the tables so that they take advantage of the landscape scheme helps to create an outdoor "room" environment. Arrange the tables up against a stand of trees or curve of bushes
OR
for the "Star-Studded" Evening,
using phosphorescent paint, do your own pop art version of the solar system on large sheet of canvas; suspend them from tall poles grouped around the tables.

TABLE CENTERPIECE AND DECORATIONS:
* ★ Candle with glass hurricane stencilled with stars
* ★ Small bouquets of multicolored flowers in two-inch square bud vases accented with a star cutout on each side
* ★ Star-shaped platters for dinner plates

SPECIAL DETAILS:
* ★ The Astronomical Society of the Pacific puts out "Tapes of the Night Sky" that include easy-to-follow instructions, star maps and a reading list

FAVORS:
* ★ Photograph (with plywood crescent moon prop) in lucite frame lettered with "A Star-Studded Affair" and date

ENTERTAINMENT:
* ★ Rent, borrow or purchase a high quality telescope for star-gazing.
* ★ Bring in one, or several authorities to provide in-depth but entertaining background on different aspects of astronomy and astrology

MUSIC:
* ★ A pre-recorded tape of songs that make reference to the stars or the moon (i.e., "Blue Moon," "Stardust," "Fly Me to the Moon," "Are the Stars Out Tonight?")

MENU

Baked brie in a crescent moon-shaped pastry
with star decorative accents
Orion's beef tenderloin with Big Dipper sauce (bordelaise)
Jupiter salad (red leaf lettuce, mandarin oranges, red onion)
with honey citrus dressing
Buttered leeks
Milky Way duchesse potatoes
Star and crescent-shaped chocolate gingerbread cookies
decorated with real silver dust

The "Flower Ladies" Weekend

What better reason to stage a weekend gathering than as a reunion of friends who all share a specific common interest? While at the same time providing an opportunity for wives and mothers to "get away"—from children, family and work demands. The following house party combines the best of all worlds—friendship, dedicated hobby, relaxation, stimulating symposiums, architectural walking tours—in a bucolic setting in the midst of an Indian summer. Additionally, playing on the different sites around the property for meal-taking provides a break from the location where the flower arranging and symposiums take place.

The "Flower Ladies" arrive bearing tins of homemade goodies, mirroring a nostalgic tradition in gracious entertaining—cheese straws, peanut brittle, Benne lemon bits, shortbread, salted pecans, Russian teacakes. They leave with many more in memories to savor—a witty Halloween "ghost," late night chats before someone begs "lights out" and the tidbits and trade secrets that are a part of flower arranging.

THEME: *The "Flower Ladies" Weekend*

ATTIRE: Casual, sensible and comfortable

INVITATION DESCRIPTION:
* Three-part, with a cover sheet of Florentine marbled paper, all secured at the corner with striped silk ribbon; each day's activities recorded on fall-toned watercolor paper, the squares graduating in size (5"x5", 6"x6", 7"x7")

DECORATIONS AND PROPS:
* After the first day's picking and gathering of the surrounding flora, each guest is issued a floral assignment to be carried out prior to dinner—a room in the house, or a centerpiece for one of the meals, or a creation to complement a specific part of the decor (i.e., a painting). Thus the "decorations/props" become not only an exercise in flower arranging but a way for each guest to enjoy the talents of their friends within this weekend environment.

Activities

Friday, October 30
LATE MORNING:
Welcome to Starrsville

LUNCH: 1:30
Tailgate Picnic

AFTERNOON:
Flora and fauna gathering led by Ila and Barbara
Flower Arranging with notes on conditioning,
mechanics and materials

EVENING:
7:30 Cocktails
8:30 Shrimp Gumbo Dinner at the "Big House"

Saturday, October 31
MORNING: 10:00
Walking Tour of Covington's Historic District,
led by Bill Wilford, author of
The Glory of Covington

LUNCH: 12:30
Cabin on the Bass Pond

AFTERNOON: 2:00
Dried Flower Demonstration and Workshop
with Ed Stiffler

Tea

EVENING:
7:30 Cocktails
8:30 Dinner

Halloween Surprise!

Sunday, November 1st
MORNING: 10:00
Williamsburg Christmas decorations workshop
with Mary Sue

Tea

LUNCH: 12:00
Harvest Picnic under the pecan trees

AFTERNOON: Au Revoir

MENUS

Saturday breakfast
Orange Smoothies
Shirred Eggs with Chive Cream
Toast Fingers
Broiled Tomatoes
Sausage or Bacon

Friday dinner
Watercress Soup
Starrsville Roast Quail
Wild Rice with Pecans
Sautéed Red Peppers
Mixed Field Greens Salad
Starrsville Sticky Toffee Pudding

Sunday lunch
Chicken Hash
Batterbread
Asparagus with Lemon Zest
Grapes with Sour Cream and Brown Sugar

Camp Days

For many of us with overprogrammed weekdays, most of our entertaining takes place on the weekends—with time to see to details, space and grounds to play in, and a casual, laid-back feeling that just lets things flow naturally. Oftentimes, a house party provides sufficient entertainment on its own; but sooner or later you'll opt to include a "supporting cast." If the guests are chosen for their sense of humor quotient, this just might be your opportunity to do a tongue-in-cheek play on the nostalgic days of yesteryear.

Here's a morning-to-night party schedule that will give those poor city dwellers a chance to breathe the fresh country air, meet a "rowing machine" that's not in a health club and ponder just how long ago, and with whom, they had their last hayride. And with a bus to "leave the driving to," all the guests will truly be happy campers.

Day's Schedule:
The chartered mini-bus, with "Camp Wannabe" banner on the sides, boards all guests in the city at 8:00 a.m. Saturday. Freshly-brewed coffee, sausage biscuits, yogurt and granola are served during the hour and a half drive to the country. Upon arrival all guests are divided into two teams: "tadpoles" and "turtles"— for the day-long "camp activities." Then everyone heads to the canoes for the paddle trip down the Alcovy River. The canoes are stocked with homemade pumpkin muffins and fresh juices, just the right size, so guests don't miss a beat paddling. Then back to the house for "Camper's Demise" (Bloody Mary's) and a basket lunch.

The afternoon is taken up with a decathalon of games, followed by a hayride all around the property as night approaches. (The pig roast and barbecue supper, for which the hay truck serves to ferry guests, should ideally take place in a different location than lunch and the games). Roasting s'mores around a campfire, accompanied by camp songs and ghost stories, is the finale to the evening. All aboard at 10:30 p.m. for the ride back to the city.

THEME: *Camp Days*

ATTIRE: T-shirts, sneakers and shorts

INVITATION DESCRIPTION:

▲ Lavaliere, with whistle and attached card labeled, "Welcome to Camp Wannabe." The few necessary details are noted on cloth tape to resemble a name tag—date, time and place to meet bus, and time it will arrive back in the city, host, party location and phone number.

DECORATIONS AND PROPS:

▲ Ten-foot banner lettered "Welcome to Camp Wannabe"
▲ Flag pole with pair of shorts hoisted on high
▲ Bar set up on stacked camp trunks, pasted up with old camp stickers
▲ Bartenders and staff dressed as nerd campers
▲ Dummy dressed as camp counselor in the bushes
▲ Rolled bale of hay with boot clad feet sticking out one end and gloved hands and hat coming out the other end
▲ Tents and camp gear scattered around grounds
▲ Assorted "Camp Rule" posters nailed to trees
▲ Basket lunch is served from the tailgate of a station wagon
▲ Open pit for evening's pig roast

TABLE FORMAT AND SEATING FOR BARBECUE:

▲ Picnic tables with green gingham place mats
▲ Flatware tied up in multicolor kerchiefs, personalized with party details

TABLE CENTERPIECE AND DECORATIONS:

▲ Oak and elm branches, with artichokes, cut melons and plastic frogs interspersed among leaves
▲ Popsicle stick "art sculpture" at the end of each table
▲ Canteens used for wine carafes
▲ Yellow daisies in small pottery jugs at each place setting

FAVORS:

▲ Rainbow selection of kerchiefs, personalized with "Camp Wannabe," date and location

SPECIAL DETAILS:
▲ A decathalon day and "Calcutta" organized around yard games of bygone days: i.e., baseball, potato sack race, three-legged race, horseshoes, "watermelon wobble"

ENTERTAINMENT:
▲ A professional storyteller to spin yarns and chilling stories around the campfire

MUSIC:
▲ "Grass Cats" bluegrass band

MENU

BASKET LUNCH
Cornish game hen with lingonberry sauce
Wild mushroom salad
Homemade parmesan biscuits
Mixed fruit
Individual linzer tortes

BARBECUE DINNER
Barbecue pork with sauce
Cornbread sticks
Brunswick stew
Coleslaw
Grilled corn
Pecan pie
Ice cold watermelon

☞ PARTY CONCEPT

The Wonderful Wizard of Oz

Bringing out the kid in each of us—while reviving memories of a childhood favorite. Who wouldn't welcome the opportunity, especially when the videotaped shenanigans become the next evening's after-dinner entertainment?

One of the secrets of successful weekend entertaining is creating—and then nurturing—a sense of esprit de corp, particularly if guests don't know one another. Giving a specific theme to the weekend immediately implies a sense of focus, further enhanced by involvement in a project. First, the do-it-yourself costume design, then the video.

If the weekend location isn't too far from everyone's hometown, this afternoon format—each couple invites a couple, or two, of their intimates who aren't known by the other guests and host—provides a creative and often overlooked alternative for ensuring a dynamic guest list.

THEME: *The Wonderful Wizard of Oz*

ATTIRE: Comfortable and skimpy—costume fixings will be supplied

INVITATION DESCRIPTION:
❖ 3' x 6" yellow brick road folding to 4" x 6"; party details, including map to destination, are printed in oversized letters covering all 3 feet of invitation.

DECORATIONS AND PROPS:
❖ Yellow fabric "brick road" leading from parking area and meandering through grounds to Emerald City where dinner is served
❖ Staked signs along yellow brick road, starting with Kansas and continuing to Emerald City
❖ Scarecrows scattered through grounds
❖ Mechanical "Toto" dog that darts out of bushes to surprise guests

- Beloved phrases from the movie—"Surrender Dorothy," "I don't think we're in Kansas anymore," "Lions and Tigers and Bears," "I'm melting!"—tacked on trees
- Tin man props holding large trays of cheese biscuits scattered through cocktail area

TABLE FORMAT AND SEATING:
- Tables are arranged inside "Emerald City," which is created from corrugated boxing, or foam core, painted green and detailed with whimsical buildings
- Round tables, with five tiers of cloth creating a rainbow impression
- Multi-colored fiesta ware plates and dishes
- Yellow napkins fanning out of wine goblets
- Buffet table repeats rainbow effect with five-tiered cloths; large, stuffed lion in middle of table; all baskets and serving containers in heart shape

TABLE CENTERPIECE AND DECORATIONS:
- Straw scattered on table and baskets filled with sunflowers

FAVORS:
- Heart-shaped red hots tied in pouch accented with a "And Toto too" pin

SPECIAL DETAILS:
- Make-your-own video with guests as movie characters: Costume fixings are provided by the host for the 30-minute sequence that he has chosen. With the original film to refer to, guests create their own character's attire. A professional director (i.e., from local high school or theater group) directs the cast in this parody which is then shown the following evening.

ENTERTAINMENT:
- Original *Wizard of Oz* playing on movie screen or VCR in living room

MUSIC:
- Hoe-down Country-Western

MENU

Lion-shaped cheese biscuits served during cocktails
Chicken and shrimp jambalaya
Herb grilled bread
Tossed "Kansas field greens" salad
Shoe-shaped cookies with red glitter

Edwardian Hunting Party

The Edwardians never did anything in a small way—their dinners were eight courses long (not including dessert or "pudding") and Edward VII and his friends were known to bag 4,000 pheasant on a four-day shoot.

While neither eight courses nor 4,000 pheasant exactly mirror today's lifestyles, the Edwardians do provide some entertaining alternatives for fall hunting weekends. Thus, what follows is a close rendition of house partying at the turn of the century. A bit of fantasy, for sure, but present day alternatives can be substituted—or let some of the ideas serve as a point of departure for planning a creative fall shoot that recalls some civilized traditions of yore (like afternoon tea). Of course, climate limitations will also have a bearing on the wardrobes of the weekend; many parts of the South, for instance, will be too warm for any more than shirt sleeves at this time.

THEME: *Edwardian Hunting Party*

ATTIRE: One was never seen in the same set of clothes twice and every aspect of the day was an opportunity for dressing "to the nines"—ladies wore an elegant velvet or silk suit for breakfast, tweeds for lunch and the two drives in the afternoon, an extravagant gown for tea and a satin or brocade full-length evening dress for the ball the first evening (jewels were also very much in evidence). Men complemented the ladies in dress, but their hunting code prescribed "plus twos or plus fours" (knickers) with long socks, ties and jackets when in the fields.

INVITATION DESCRIPTION:
✠ Written in gold ink on heavy ecru card stock, the invitation would be placed within a shallow gift box; then wrapped in royal purple velvet, tied with a white satin ribbon and accented with silk ruby red roses.

TABLE FORMAT AND SEATING:

✠ Large, hardwood oblong table covered with a royal purple damask cloth with overlay of finely meshed gold tulle

✠ Place cards and menu cards of heavy ecru stock, penned in gold ink

✠ Small garland of light lavender roses across back of each gilded ballroom chair

TABLE CENTERPIECE AND DECORATIONS:

✠ A mass of gold tulle creating a cloud effect down the center of the table, interspersed with generous pyramids of assorted fruit grouped on footed compotes and ruby red roses, massed in silver bowls

ENTERTAINMENT:

✠ It was the custom to save the last night for amateur dramatics, in which all were expected to participate. Thus, elaborate rehearsals became an integral part of the four-day shoot and the way that one amused oneself when not shooting or dressing.

MUSIC:

✠ Chamber orchestra

SAMPLE MENU
To be recorded on menu cards
Lunch was five courses; dinner was eight courses

Green turtle soup (hot)
Jellied consommé (cold)
Broiled trout
Filet of sole with mornay sauce
Saddle of mutton
Grapefruit sorbet
Quail, or game in season
Oysters on toast points
Bombe glacé
Coffee with chocolates

Toasts

"May you be Hung, Drawn and Quartered!
Yes—hung with diamonds
Drawn in a coach and four
And quartered in the best houses in the land."

"A toast to our host
From the short and tall of us,
May he live to be
The guest of all of us."

House Rules

The nicest place on earth to go
　　Is not the south of France
It's not the sunny Palm Beach shore
　　And Everglades to dance
It's not in Rome where tourists should
　　'Do as the Romans do'
It's just a piece of heaven here
　　In a house they call "Canoe."

There's all that anyone could want
　　Right here among the Pines
You're free to chase a golf ball 'round
　　You're free to taste the wines.
You're free to go out shopping and
　　You're free to hit the pools —
But while you're here, we must insist
　　You follow certain rules.

We do not wear a frown at all
　　Inspite of rotten scores
And if you've had an awful day
　　With eights instead of fours
We will not have you sulking here
　　No lamentations blue
No litany of shame allowed
　　In a house we call "Canoe."

Don't tell us all your rotten luck
　　Of greens with unfair humps
Just keep those bogies to yourself
　　We all must take our lumps —
Feel free to bring your score card and
　　Peruse it on the deck
But if you tell us hole by hole
　　We'll surely wring your neck!

Responsibility for each
　　And each will toe the line
If you will paddle your canoe
　　Then I will paddle mine
Aladdin's lamp is ours to use
　　And wishes will come true
We'll spend this time of happy days
　　In a house they call "Canoe."

—Written by Francie Rankin for Nancy and George Lyles

The PARDEE GUIDE Series

Bettie Bearden Pardee

GREAT ENTERTAINING
1,000 Party Tips and Timesavers
$11.95 / ISBN 1-56145-001-4
An overview of entertaining essentials
providing a wealth of knowledge on party planning
and party giving.

GREAT WEEKEND ENTERTAINING
An Essential Companion for Fun-Loving Hosts and Guests
$9.95 / ISBN 1-56145-022-7
An easy-to-use guide which makes weekend entertaining
memorable and manageable for hosts and guests.

GREAT THEME PARTIES FOR THE NINETIES
$9.95 / ISBN 1-56145-030-8
Illuminating details for planning and presenting theme
parties with pizzazz—from invitations to decorations,
guest lists and table designs—whether for a simple
gathering or an elaborate affair.

Available from your local bookseller, gift shop, or from
PEACHTREE PUBLISHERS   (800)241-0113

Index